SUBMARINE INSIGNIA

& SUBMARINE SERVICES
OF THE WORLD

Lieutenant-Commander W M Thornton
MBE RD* RNR (Rtd)

with the collaboration of
Capitán de Navio Gustavo Conde, Argentine Navy

LEO COOPER
London

First published in 1997 by
Leo Cooper
190 Shaftesbury Avenue, London WC2H 8JL
an imprint of
Pen & Sword Books Ltd,
47 Church Street, Barnsley, South Yorkshire S70 2AS

A CIP catalogue record for this book is available from the British Library

ISBN 0 85052 536 5

Printed in Singapore by Kyodo Printing Co (Singapore) Pte Ltd

CONTENTS

Foreword

In this book an attempt has been made to depict all the insignia that have been worn and are being worn by qualified submariners world-wide. No doubt readers will come across insignia that do not appear but these will, for the most part, be variation in manufacture, size and material. This reference should therefore, at the very least, serve to identify the country of origin and give relevant background information. New insignia will be produced as new submarine forces are formed. Hopefully these will be included in a revised volume to follow at some later date.

Various insignia have been produced, the authenticity of which, at this stage, cannot be verified. These are shown for information, and in some cases, assumptions made.

As an additional aid to identification, unofficial designs, if actually worn, are included. Some of these were the fore-runners of authorized insignia that were to follow.

Where actual examples of the insignia are not available, or where the illustrations are not suitable for reproduction, the author has prepared drawings for identification purposes. Note that the illustrations are not to scale.

ABBREVIATIONS USED IN THE TEXT

SS   Conventionally powered(diesel/electric) submarine
SSC   Conventionally powered (diesel/electric) small coastal submarine
SSK   Conventionally powered (diesel/electric) submarine with anti-submarine warfare capability
SSB   Conventionally powered (diesel/electric) ballistic missile submarine
SSG   Conventionally powered (diesel/electric) cruise missile submarine
SSN   Nuclear powered hunter-killer attack submarine
SSBN   Nuclear powered ballistic missile submarine
SSGN   Nuclear powered cruise missile submarine
SDV   Swimmer delivery vehicle
          (The above refer only to post-1945 construction)
SLBM   Submarine launched ballistic missile
SSM   Surface to surface missile
USM   Underwater to surface missile
A/S   Anti-submarine
ASW   Anti-submarine warfare
ICBM   Intrecontinental ballistic missile
NM   Nautical miles

SOVIET SUBMARINE CLASSIFICATION

NATO terminology is used in the text for most Soviet or ex-Soviet submarine classes.

SS	*Quebec*	SSB	*Golf*
	Whiskey	SSG	*Juliet*
	Romeo	SSBN	*Hotel*
	Zulu		*Yankee*
	Foxtrot		*Delta*
SSK	*Tango*		*Typhoon*
	Kilo	SSGN	*Echo*
SSN	*November*		*Charlie*
	Victor		*Papa*
	Alpha		*Oscar*
	Sierra		
	Mike		

EXPLANATION OF
EARLY SUBMARINE TYPES

Early submarine types were usually known after their inventors, some of these were:

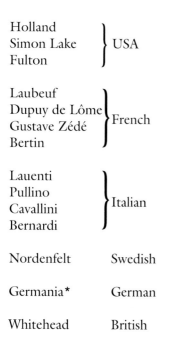

Holland
Simon Lake } USA
Fulton

Laubeuf
Dupuy de Lôme
Gustave Zédé } French
Bertin

Lauenti
Pullino
Cavallini } Italian
Bernardi

Nordenfelt   Swedish

Germania*   German

Whitehead   British

* This is named after the shipyard.

Note that early submarines were termed submarine torpedo boats, consequently they are always referred to as boats, rather than ships.

ALBANIA

SUBMARINE SERVICE

The Albanian submarine branch was formed in 1960 with the transfer of two *Whiskey* Class submarines (SS) from the USSR. When in 1961, after the split with Albania, the Soviet Union attempted to withdraw from its bases two further *Whiskey* Class submarines, then in Albanian ports, these were seized, thus doubling the Albanian submarine strength.

One submarine was deleted in 1976 and shortly thereafter another one relegated to harbour service. The remaining boats, which are the only significant vessels in the navy, are assumed to be operational.

SUBMARINE INSIGNIA

Very little information is available from Albania. In line with their Chinese Communist patrons, all ranks and insignia, apart from the red star cap badge, were abolished about 1966 and an universal Chairman-Mao style uniform adopted. Later, following the Chinese lead, the Navy changed to a more traditional uniform based almost entirely on the Chinese style.

After the collapse of Communism in March, 1992, more conventional uniforms and insignia of rank were introduced. A submarine badge made its appearance about early 1993. It consisted of the image of a conventional submarine measuring 92mm x 18mm facing the wearer's right. It was crudely embroidered in light grey thread on a dark blue background which usually followed the profile of the submarine. Further details are, at this stage, unavailable.

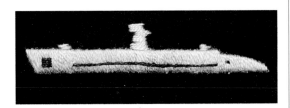

*Albanian submarine insignia
introduced early 1993.*

ALGERIA

SUBMARINE SERVICE

The Algerian Submarine Force was formed in January, 1982, with the delivery of a Soviet *Romeo* Class submarine (SS). A second submarine of the same class was delivered the following year. Both boats were on loan for a five year period and were subsequently returned to the Soviet Union. In 1987 a *Kilo* Class submarine (SSK) was purchased from the Soviet Union and was followed by a second one in 1988. These two modern submarines are likely to constitute the Algerian submarine force for the foreseeable future.

SUBMARINE INSIGNIA

In 1992 official sources indicated that no formal insignia was authorized. Since then various unsubstantiated reports have rumoured that a submarine badge has been 'seen' but no details have emerged.

ARGENTINA

SUBMARINE SERVICE

Though experiments with a small electric powered vessel were reported in 1906/7, it was not until 1927 that Argentina ordered its first submarines. The new vessels, three in number, with a surface displacement of 775 tons, were purchased from Italy, and were based on the Italian Navy's *Mameli* Class. Named *Salta, Sante Fé* and *Santiago del Estero* after Argentine provinces, these became traditional names for Argentinian submarines. They served for nearly three decades; the *Salta*, the last to be withdrawn, served until 1960.

In the same year as *Salta* was decommissioned the United States transferred two wartime-built *Balao* class submarines (SS), of 1,816 tons surface displacement, to Argentina. They became the *Sante Fé* and *Santiago del Estero*. Eleven years later both were replaced by two modernised *Balao* Class submarines (*Guppy 1A* and *Guppy 11*). The names adopted were the same as the names of the two submarines that they had replaced. The *Sante Fé* was later to gain notoriety when she became the first war loss in the Falklands conflict. She was disabled off South Georgia on the 26 April, 1982, by missiles fired from a Lynx helicopter from

HMS *Brilliant*, and was subsequently beached to become a total loss.

In the late 1960s two 209 class — 1200 type submarines (SSK) of 980 tons surface displacement were ordered from West Germany. They were built in sections at Kiel and shipped to Argentina for assembly. Both were commissioned in 1974 and were named *Salta* and *San Luis*. Plans for an additional two type 209s were dropped in favour of a further order from West Germany of six of the more advanced TR 1700 type (SSK) displacing 2,116 tons surfaced. The first two of this class, the *Sante Cruz* and the *Santa Juan*, were constructed in West Germany and sailed for Argentina in 1984 and 1985 respectively. The remaining vessels, the first two of which have been named *Santiago del Estero* and *Sante Fé*, are being constructed in Argentina with West German help. It is likely that the class will be reduced to a total of five boats. At the time of writing Argentina has in commission two type TR 1700 Class and two type 209 *Salta* Class.

SUBMARINE INSIGNIA

The original submarine badge, proposed by Presidential Decree on 16 December, 1933, was based on the design of the Italian-built *Mameli* Class submarines. It faced the wearer's right as did all subsequent badges.

It came in three grades, one for officers, one for senior ratings and one for junior ratings. The officer's insignia, which was of gilt metal, bore an enamel oval device centrally located below the conning tower. This consisted of three equally spaced horizontal segments of light blue, white and light blue with a gilt sunburst in the centre of the white segment. The senior rating's insignia was similar but made of brass with an anchor within the oval. Junior ratings wore a cloth badge on the sleeve. The ovals were surrounded by a representation of a rope. Both the metal badges had horizontal pin fastenings and measured 75mm x 20mm.

In 1945 the officer's badge was modified by replacing the central oval with the national coat-of-arms in full colour enamel. In 1969 the senior ratings badge was similarly modified but was now made in silver. At the same time it was authorized for all ranks below commissioned officer.

A small version of the submarine badge 37mm long can be worn on mess kit or worn at sea as a beret badge. The submarine insignia is also produced in yellow or white embroidery on navy blue cloth for wear on the sea service jacket. Gold or silver embroidery versions are also produced, probably for private purchase.

The submarine insignia was originally worn on the left breast below the pocket on the blue uniform or above the pocket on the khaki and

ARGENTINA

white uniforms. Foreign submarine qualification badges are permitted to be worn below the Argentine insignia by personnel who have successfully completed submarine courses in other countries. From 1970 officers were authorized to wear the submarine insignia on the right breast.

Two new qualification badges were introduced about 1993/4. The first is the Submarine Support Badge and is worn only by commissioned ranks who serve ashore but who are attached to the submarine service. Originally restricted to medical officers specializing in underwater medicine (they formerly wore the standard officer's badge) it now includes naval engineering constructors and architects. The badge is the same design and size as that for sea-going officers but the central device is all gilt and not in coloured enamel.

The second and most individual of Argentinan submarine badges came with the appointment of Senior Chief Petty Officer of the Submarine Force. Based at Submarine Headquarters this senior rating wears a special badge depicting the rating's type submarine badge but on a blue enamel field within a gilt 'roped' frame measuring 45mm x 29mm overall.

The cap tallies of ratings serving in submarines bear the name of the submarine prefixed by the letters 'ARS' (*Armada de la Republica Argentina*) or in the case of the submarine school the words 'A. R. A. ESC. DE SUBMARINOS'.

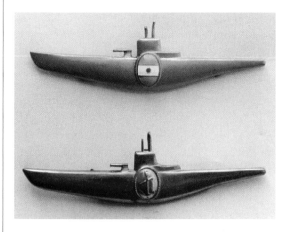

Argentine submarine
qualification insignia first
pattern.
Top: officers 1933 to 1945.
Bottom: senior ratings 1933
to 1969.

Argentine submarine
qualification insignia second
pattern.
Top: officers 1945.
Bottom: senior ratings 1969.

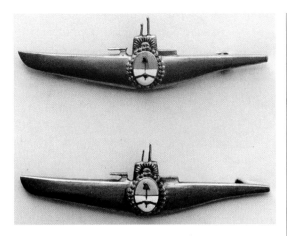

Argentine submarine
support badge 1993/94.

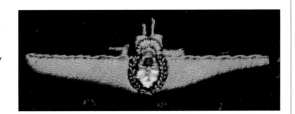

Officer's cloth submarine
insignia worn on sea service
jacket. A similar insignia in
white embroidery is worn by
ratings.

Miniature insignia worn by submarine officers on
mess dress and berets. It is also found on tie slides.

AUSTRALIA

SUBMARINE SERVICE

The Australian Submarine service commenced with the launching by Vickers of the Submarine AE1 on 22 May, 1913, followed by the launching of AE2 on 18 June, 1913. Both were of the British E Class and had a surface displacement of 725 tons.

The two small submarines made the 13,000-mile voyage from Barrow to Sydney under their own power shortly before the commencement of World War I.

AEI disappeared on 14 September, 1914, off New Britain while in support of operations in New Guinea. AE2 sailed with the second AIF to the Mediterranean on the last day of 1914.

On 25 April, 1915, she forced her way through the Dardanelles and five days later crippled a Turkish cruiser with torpedoes. Shortly after the attack AE2 lost control due to damage caused by currents and was forced to surface. Attacked by an enemy destroyer, she was compelled to scuttle herself and her company became prisoners of war. The loss of the two submarines constituted the only RAN losses of World War I.

In 1919 all six boats of the RN J Class were transferred to the RAN. These vessels had a surface displacement of 1,210 tons and were completed between 1915 and 1917. Their service in the RAN was short-lived; none were kept in commission for more than three years.

In 1924 it was decided to order two new submarines from Britain to replace the obsolete J Class. HMAS *Oxley* was launched in June, 1926, and HMAS *Otway* in October of the same year. Both were of the 1,475 tons surface displacement O Class. They arrived in Australian waters in 1929 just before the Great Depression of Australia. When Depression came, both submarines fell victims of the economic situation and were transferred to the RN in April, 1931.

In 1943 a Dutch submarine, K-9, manned by the RN with a section of RAN volunteers, was commissioned into the RAN but was paid off within nine months. No further submarines were to serve in the RAN until after World War II.

From 1956 to 1969 the RN based its 4th Submarine Squadron (comprising three to four submarines) at Sydney to assist the RAN in anti-submarine warfare training.

The reinstatement of the Australian submarine service was heralded in January, 1963, when the Minster of the Navy announced that four

Oberon Class submarines (SS) were to be built for the RAN: HMA submarines *Onslow, Otway, Ovens* and *Oxley* were subsequently launched between 1965 and 1968 and commissioned between 1967 and 1969. Two further boats HMA Submarines *Orion* and *Otama* were launched in 1974 and 1975 and commissioned in 1977 and 1978. Known as the *Otway* Class these six submarines comprised the 1st RAN submarine squadron. They have a surface displacement of 2,186 tons. Six were modernized by Vickers at Cockatoo Island between 1977 and 1985, and were fitted with USM upgrading them to SSK. *Oxley, Otway* and *Ovens* were deleted in 1992, 1994 and 1995 respectively.

On 18 May, 1987, the Australian Defence Minister announced that the replacements for the *Otway* Class would be the Type 471 Swedish submarine (SSK) designed by Kockums Marine. To be known as the *Collins* Class they are to have a surface displacement of 3,051 tons and will be constructed in Australia. The first of the class HMAS *Collins* was commissioned in January, 1995. The remainder, HMA submarines *Farncomb, Waller, Dechaineux, Sheean* and *Rankin,* should all be in service by 1999.

SUBMARINE INSIGNIA

The Australian submarine insignia was authorized by Australian Navy Order 411/64 promulgated on 25 July, 1966. It was officially described as a 'gold plated gilding metal brooch depicting two dolphins, nose to nose supporting a crown' and is the same for both officers and ratings. The first issues were made on 17 December, 1966. It is produced in two sizes; the dimension of the standard size is 72mm x 21mm and the miniature, for wear on mess dress, measures 51mm x 16mm. Both types are secured to the uniform by clutch fasteners. Gold wire embroidered versions are produced for private purchase. The insignia is worn on the left breast above medal ribbons. On 19 August, 1987, a similar yellow embroidered badge on dark cloth was authorized by Australian Submarine Temporary Memorandum (ASSTM 50/87), to be worn on working jackets by all qualified personnel.

For officers the qualification requirement is six months' sea-service after completion of training. For ratings it is granted after training and passing a submarine sea test normally held after sixteen weeks' service in a submarine.

Junior ratings wear cap ribbons bearing the submarine's name prefixed by the letters HMAS in exactly the same manner as for surface ships and establishments.

Australian submarine
qualification badges worn by
all ranks from 1966.
Top: insignia normally worn.
Centre: miniature insignia
for wear on mess dress.
Bottom: cloth variation worn
on working rig.

AUSTRIA-HUNGARY

SUBMARINE SERVICE

The Austro-Hungarian Navy formed its submarine arm in 1908. In that
year four boats were ordered, two American Lake type designated U1
and U2 and two Improved Holland type from Vickers Ltd designated
U3 and U4. The following year two further boats designated U5 and
U6 were ordered from Krupps Germania yard at Kiel. All six were delivered in 1910.

At the outbreak of the World War I Austria-Hungary had the afore-
mentioned six submarines plus five building at Krupps. The new class
was to be designated U7 to U11, but with the intervention of the war
they were incorporated into the German Navy.

Five classes of submarines, totalling fourteen boats, were added to
the Navy during the war. Most were Austro-Hungarian built, but some
were acquired from Germany. The boats built in wartime were all designated by roman numerals as follows: XV completed 1914, XVII and XI
completed 1915, XXI and XXII completed in 1916, XXVII, XXIX and
XXXII also completed in 1916 and XL, XII, XLII and XVLII completed

in 1918. Another thirteen boats were under construction but never completed. All were small coastal types, the largest having a surface displacement of 516 tons, though the majority were half this size. In addition a number of German U-Boats were transferred to the A/H Flag, but in some cases they continued to be manned by German crews.

Some fifteen or twenty submarines were lost during the war and on capitulation the remainder were interned in Italian ports.

Eventually a few were incorporated into the French and Italian Navies (one was allocated to Bulgaria but was later transferred to France). The remainder were broken up under Allied supervision.

SUBMARINE INSIGNIA

The Austro-Hungarian submarine insignia was authorized on 15 April, 1910. It was to be worn on the left side (breast pocket) of the fleet tunic, blue shirt, white jacket or cotton jacket below all other medals and decorations. It could only be worn by personnel while actually serving in submarines.

It was manufactured in pressed matt silver finish metal for officers and pressed plain white metal for ratings. The insignia was secured by a 12mm pin and measured 36mm wide by 56mm high. There was also a sew-on version. The design consisted of a fouled anchor with the letters UB on either side of the shank.

Cap ribbons for sailors serving in submarines bore the inscription 'S. M. UNTERSEEBOOT I', etc, the appropriate boat number in roman numerals being at the end.

When Austria became part of the Third Reich in 1938, Austrians electing to serve in the newly constituted armed forces were allowed to wear their World War I medals; these included the few who were entitled to the submarine badge. A limited number of Austro-Hungarian Navy insignia were, therefore, produced in 1938 using the original tools.

Reproductions have been seen in brass and also in white metal non-voided. These usually have thin pin fixings.

Austro-Hungary submarine insignia authorized 15 April, 1910. Manufactured in matt silver for officers and in white metal for ratings.

BELGIUM

At the end of World War I, two of the 105 surrendered U-Boats allocated to Great Britain were given to Belgium. These boats were never put into service and were broken up between 1922 and 1923.

BRAZIL

SUBMARINE SERVICE

The Brazilian Navy created its submarine arm with the commissioning of three Italian-built Fiat Laurenti type submarines on 17 July, 1914. These three boats designated F1, F3 and F5 had a surface displacement of 250 tons.

It was not until July, 1929, fifteen years later, that a fourth submarine was commissioned. She was the *Humaita* of the Ansaldo type. Built in Italy, she closely resembled the Italian Navy *Balilla* Class of 1,450 tons surface displacement with a mine-laying capability.

The three original submarines were replaced in 1937 with the delivery of three-Italian built *Odero-Terni-Orlando* type submarines. These were similar to the Italian Navy *Perla* class of 615 tons surface displacement. They were designated the T Class and named *Tupi*, *Tamoio* and *Timbira*.

These three boats along with the *Humaita* comprised the Brazilian submarine force during World War II. Brazil entered the war, on the Allied side, on 22 August, 1942, following the torpedoing of five Brazilian ships off the coast of Bahia.

The flotilla was reduced to three boats when the *Humaita* was paid off in the early 1950s. However, in 1957 the United States loaned Brazil two *Gato* Class submarines (SS) for five years under the Mutual Defence Assistance programme. These vessels received the names of *Humaita* (ex-USS *Muskillunge*) and *Riachuelo* (ex-USS *Paddle*). Both had been completed in 1943 and had a surface displacement of 1,525 tons. These vessels were replaced in 1963 by two more former USN submarines this time of the *Balao* Class (SS) and named *Bahia* (ex-USS *Plaice*) and *Rio Grande Do Sul* (ex-USS *Sand Lance*).

Between 1972 and 1973 Brazil purchased five ex-USN *Guppy II* type submarines (SS) built between 1945 and 1946. These became the *Bahia* (ex-USS *Sea Leopard*), *Ceara*, (ex-USS *Amberjack*), *Guan Abara* (ex-USS *Dogfish*), *Rio De Janeiro* (ex-USS *Odax*) and *Rio Grande Do Sul* (ex-USS *Grampus*). The two *Balao* Class submarines were deleted as their namesakes came into service.

1973 saw the purchase of two more ex-USN submarines. These were of the *Guppy III* type (SS) and had been completed in 1946. They were given the names *Amazonas* (ex-USS *Greenfish*) and *Goiaz* (ex-USS *Trumpetfish*).

The submarine arm was again increased in 1973 with the commissioning of new British-built *Oberon* submarines (SS) named the *Humaita* and a further two, the *Tonelero* and *Riachuelo*, commissioned in 1977, again replacing older submarines of the same name. These submarines were later upgraded to SSK status.

The latest boats are the German 209 Class (type 1400) (SSK). They have a displacement of 1,260 tons and are armed with eight 21in torpedo tubes and are designated the *Tupi* Class. The first was constructed in Germany and her three sisters were or are building, under licence, in Brazil. *Tupi* was commissioned in 1989 and *Tamoio* was commissioned in 1994. *Timbira* and *Tabajos* are due to be commissioned in 1996 and 1999 respectively.

Further plans include two 'stretched' versions of the 209 class, to be named *Tocantins* and *Tamandare*, and designs are being considered for a nuclear propelled attack submarine (SSN), but financial restrictions may mean that this project will be long-term.

At the time of writing (1996) the submarine arm consists of two 209 *Tupi* Class (SSK) and two building and three *Oberon* Class (SSK).

SUBMARINE INSIGNIA

The Brazilian submarine insignia was instituted by Decree No. 19.747 on 10 March, 1931. The design is based on the first class of submarine to serve in the Navy. This was the F Class which came into service in 1941.

The device, which faces its wearer's left, is the same for both officers and ratings. It is manufactured in gilt coloured pressed metal, though heavier metal variations are available. The insignia comes in one size only and is 83mm long. It is worn by officers on the left breast above the uniform pocket and by ratings on the right breast. In both cases it is secured to the uniform with two clutch fasteners. A variation occurs in some insignia with the area between the periscopes being solid; normally it is voided. An unofficial miniature also exists.

Two other versions exist. Officers, at their own expense, may wear gold wire embroidered badges and a velcro-backed cloth cotton embroidered device has been available for use on some forms of working dress. A third variation has also been reported, insignia produced in silver coloured metal. No confirmation has, as yet, emerged that this is official.

Brazilian submarine
qualification insignia, all
ranks from 10 March,
1931.

Brazilian submarine
qualification insignia
embroidered in gold wire.

Brazilian submarine
qualification insignia
embroidered in yellow cloth.

BULGARIA

SUBMARINE SERVICE

The first Bulgarian submarine was the ex Austro-Hungarian XVIII, ceded in 1919 but never put into service. Shortly after the transfer it was taken over by the French Navy. The actual start of the submarine arm took place between 1959 and 1960 when the Soviet Union delivered three MIV type coastal submarines (SS) to Bulgaria. These had a surface displacement of 205 tons and were designated M1, M2 and M3. They continued in service until 1967.

In 1958 two Soviet *Whiskey* Class submarines (SS) were commissioned as the *Pobeda* and *Slava*. In 1972 they were replaced by two Soviet *Romeo* Class (SS) which were given the same names. These two boats were scrapped in 1990 and 1993. A third *Romeo* was commissioned in 1985 and a fourth one in 1986. Named *Nadezhda* and *Slava*, they constitute the present Bulgarian Submarine Force.

Submarine Insignia

Though Bulgaria had no operational submarines before 1959 a silver-plated submarine badge was said to have been worn between 1940 and 1944. It took the form of a submarine (U-Boat profile) facing to the wearer's right and measured 72mm x 22mm. It can only have been unofficial and if worn would probably have been for volunteers serving with the German Navy.

Bulgaria played only a small part in World War II, allowing Germany to occupy her territory on the promise of new lands from her neighbours. She never declared war on the USSR, though she did declare war on Great Britain and the United States of America. After the Soviet occupation she threw in her lot with the Allies.

The official Bulgarian submarine insignia was introduced in August, 1984, being the thirtieth anniversary of the foundation of the Submarine Division (primarily formed to embrace trainee submariners in the USSR). The device is made of brass with coloured enamelled details. It is shield-shaped with the upper part bearing the War Ensign and the lower part being plain light blue. A submarine, in gold, bearing a central red star facing the wearer's left is located in the middle. The shield measures 30mm x 39mm and the submarine overlaps being 38mm long.

The insignia is worn on the right breast by all qualified ranks on duty and in the reserve.

A similar badge but lacking the red star on the War Ensign and with dark blue on the lower segment is available for presentation to friends and guests. It is not worn on uniform.

In common with all Bulgarian insignia the red star was dropped in 1992. The present submarine insignia, therefore, lacks the red star on the War Ensign and on the submarine's hull.

Bulgarian submarine insignia introduced in 1984. The red stars on the War Ensign and on the submarine's hull were removed in 1992.

Bulgarian submarine insignia, probably unofficial, said to have been worn between 1940 and 1944.

Unofficial Bulgarian submarine insignia for friends and guests. The red star was removed in 1992.

CANADA

SUBMARINE SERVICE

Canada's first submarines were two Holland type boats, CC1 and CC2. They were built in Seattle for Chile but purchased by Canada in 1914 just before the outbreak of World War I. They were small boats of about 310 tons surface displacement and were used for coastal patrols. Both were disposed of in 1920.

In 1919 the United Kingdom Government presented Canada with two H Class submarines, H14 and H15, which were re-designated CH14 and CH15. However, due to financial restraints, both were deleted in 1922.

It was not until well after World War II that the submarine branch was re-established. In 1961 the US *Balao* Class submarine USS *Burrfish* was purchased and renamed HMCS *Grilse*. Her function was to act as a training target for anti-submarine warfare, a role previously undertaken by Royal Navy submarines on loan to Canada. She remained in service until 1969, being replaced by the US *Tench* Class submarine USS *Argonaut*.

Renamed HMCS *Rainbow*, she continued in service until 1974. The post-war ex-USN submarines were all classified SS.

In the meantime three *Oberon* Class submarines had been ordered from British Yards in order to carry on the task of anti-submarine warfare training. The first, HMCS *Ojibwa*, entered service in 1965, the second, HMCS *Onodaga*, entered service in 1967 and the third, HMCS *Okanagan*, entered service in 1968. These three 'O' boats constitute the present strength of the Canadian Navy's submarine arm. The *Oberons* were originally classified SS, later upgraded to SSK.

The need to protect Canada's Arctic coastline led to tenders abroad for four submarines and possibly eight or twelve, probably nuclear powered, as they would be required to carry out under-ice patrols. Selection was scheduled for 1990 and completion dates were projected as 1995 to 1999. British or French designs were most likely to be accepted. This programme was cancelled in April, 1989, on economic grounds. In the same year the British submarine *Olympus* was acquired for static harbour training and in 1992 *Osiris* was acquired for spare-part cannibalization.

SUBMARINE INSIGNIA

With the reforming of the submarine branch of the RCN in 1961 a cloth badge depicting a single diving dolphin was authorized for qualified submariners. For officers it was produced in gold bullion on a navy blue backing. This was also worn by ratings on their number one uniforms. For working dress, ratings wore the same badge red on dark blue and for tropical uniform dark blue on white.

The badge measured 40mm high x 21mm wide. It was worn on the left sleeve immediately above rank devices in the case of officers and chief petty officers and 3in above the cuff in the case of petty officers and other ratings. Variations of size have appeared and an unofficial gilt badge was produced.

With the unification of the Canadian Forces the insignia was altered for all ranks to yellow rayon on dark green. This style was worn from 1968 to 1972. Metal versions have appeared but these are quite unofficial.

In April, 1972, the Queen approved the new Canadian Forces submarine badge. It was officially described as 'a crimson garnet wreath of laurel between two swimming dolphins in gold, above the wreath a crown, within the centre of the wreath a gold coloured maple leaf'. The device measured 82mm long x 33mm high and was of cloth material. In July, 1970, the badge was produced in metal 70mm long x 30mm high. It was secured to the uniform by two clutch fasteners. These new badges

CANADA

were worn in cloth or wire embroidery above the left breast pocket of the CF green service dress and in metal above the left breast pocket of the CF green or white short-sleeved shirt. Miniature devices were available for mess dress.

With the reintroduction of the traditional dark blue (actually black) naval uniforms, in May, 1986, the device in cloth or bullion has reverted to the left cuff, the metal badge being confined to shirts and working dress. The design has remained unaltered, though in the case of the cloth insignia the backing has been changed from dark green to the new uniform colour.

The only cap ribbons worn for submarine service bore the submarine's name. They were 'HMCS RAINBOW', 'HMCS OJIBWA', 'HMCS ONONDAGA' and 'HMCS OKANAGAN'. No cap tally was produced for HMCS *Grilse,* nor were any produced with 'HMC SUBMARINES' (in the RN manner).With the adoption of the CF green uniforms cap tallies became obsolete and have not been reintroduced for the new naval type uniforms (which began to be issued in 1985). In this uniform all members of the naval service wear peaked caps.

The Royal Canadian Sea Cadets had a submarine orientated badge, acquired after successfully completing a basic course in a naval establishment. Like all RCSC badges it was embroidered silvery white on navy blue cloth. It took the form of two dolphins nose-to-nose above which was a maple leaf and below a short scroll bearing the word 'CADET'. The backing cloth was contoured. It was intended for wear on the left breast. This badge was replaced by a sleeve device depicting an O Class submarine (facing left) below a maple leaf, again white on navy blue.

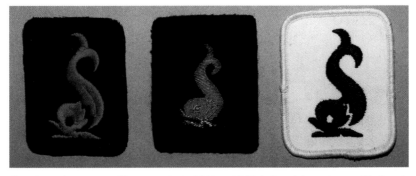

Canadian submarine qualification insignia 1961 to 1968. Left to right, ratings on No 2 and 3 uniforms, officers for normal wear and ratings for No 1 uniform, ratings tropical uniforms. Royal Canadian Navy.

Canadian submarine qualification insignia, Maritime Command, Canadian Forces (N). All ranks 1972 to 1986, dark green backing.

Canadian submarine qualification insignia, Maritime Command, Canadian Forces (N). All ranks 1968 to 1971, deep yellow on dark green backing.

Canadian submarine qualification insignia, Maritime Command, Canadian Forces (N). All ranks from May 1986, for new 'traditional' uniforms with black backing.

Canadian submarine qualification insignia in metal. All ranks for wear on specified uniforms from July, 1972.

Canadian submarine qualification insignia, miniature size, in gold wire embroidery.

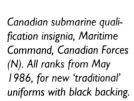

CANADA

Canadian submarine qualification insignia, probably produced unofficially, for wear by ex-submariners or for wear on dress uniforms of other services.

Royal Canadian Sea Cadet, submarine dolphin badge. First type.

Royal Canadian Sea Cadets, submarine branch badge worn on the sleeve. Second type.

CHILE

SUBMARINE SERVICE

The first Chilean submarines were built between 1915 and 1917. These were six Holland type boats constructed in the USA. Designated H1 to H6 they were originally intended for delivery to Great Britain but were interned in the USA on the outbreak of World War I. When the USA entered the war in 1917 they were released, but Great Britain ceded them to Chile in part payment for Chilean warships building in UK yards in 1914 and appropriated by the Royal Navy. They had a surface displacement of 355 tons and were later re-named *Gualcolda, Tegualda, Rucumilla, Guale, Quidora* and *Fresia* (names of heroines who fought the Spanish invaders). Four were broken up just after the war and the remainder, amazingly, not until between 1955 and 1956.

In 1928 and 1929 three Vickers Armstrong submarines of the O Class were purchased, newly constructed, and named after the Naval heroes *Capitan O'Brien, Capitan Thomson* and *Almirante Simpson*. They had a surface displacement of 1,540 tons. In 1958 all three were discarded.

In 1959 two ex-USN *Balao* Class submarines (SS) were scheduled to replace the O Boats but they were not finally transferred until 1961. They became *Simpson* (ex-USS *Spot*) and *Thomson* (ex-USS *Springer*).

Two British *Oberon* Class submarines (SS) were then ordered and both were delivered in 1976 and were given the names of *O'Brien* and *Hyatt*. On their being commissioned, the *Balao* Class *Thomson* was paid off and used for spares. *Simpson* was similarly paid off in 1975, but re-activated in 1977, only to be finally disposed of about three years later.

Two new 209 Class (type 1300) patrol submarines (SSK) were ordered from West Germany in 1980 and arrived in Chile in 1984. Of 1,260 tons surface displacement they are armed with eight 21in torpedo tubes.

The present submarine force consists of the two 209 Class and two *Oberon* Class. A further two 209s are contemplated.

SUBMARINE INSIGNIA

On 20 July, 1918, coinciding with the arrival of the first H Class submarine, officers and ratings commenced to wear on their left breast the first submarine insignia. This device depicted a Holland type submarine facing its wearer's right and measured 60mm long. Various minor variations existed. Unofficial at first, it became authorized on 5 August, 1927, and was to be gilt for officers and aluminium for ratings. In 1929, a year after O Class submarines were purchased, a new badge in the style of this class appeared, this time facing its wearer's left. Ship's companies wore the different designs in accordance with which class they served. In 1955 the O Class design was universally adopted because it 'looked more modern'. Known in the Chilean Navy as the *Piocha,* the insignia depicts the O Class submarine with jumping stays and measures 67mm by 14.5mm. It comes in one size only and is worn by all ranks on the left breast above medal ribbons. It is fixed with lugs, pins or clutch fasteners. In 1963 a new die replaced the former one which had been lost. This resulted in some minor variations. In 1971 a new badge appeared without jumping stays but proved unpopular. These were said to have been manufactured in the United Kingdom during a visit to Portsmouth by the O Boats.

The Uniform Regulations of 25 August, 1987, reintroduced the previous design in gilt for all ranks; at the same time a frosted silver insignia of the same design was authorized for certain non-sea-going personnel attached to the submarine service. These included technicians, suppliers and medical personnel.

A special beret insignia is worn by submariners. It is officially described as 'an elliptical diadem with national heraldic flowers which surround the silhouette of an O Class submarine 38mm long. The diadem dimensions are, main axis 55mm, minor axis 40mm. Diadem and submarine (which are separate) are in gold colour'. The wreath is surmounted by a naval crown.

Chilean Navy submarine service beret badge.

Chilean submarine insignia first authorized 5 August, 1927.

Chilean submarine qualification insignia from 1955, all ranks. From top to bottom:

Insignia without jumping stays 1971 to 1987.

Insignia with jumping stays 1955 to 1971 and from 1987.

Frosted silver insignia for associated personnel from 1987.

Miniature.

PEOPLE'S REPUBLIC OF CHINA

SUBMARINE SERVICE

China first included submarines in its Navy in 1954. By the end of the 1970s the Chinese submarine fleet was the world's third largest.

Between 1954 and 1957 the Soviet Union transferred to China fourteen small coastal vessels of prewar design. Most of these were deleted by 1963. These were followed by the transfer of six Soviet *Whiskey* Class (SS) and the assembling in Chinese shipyards of a further fifteen from Soviet components. At about the same time four Soviet *Romeo* Class (SS) were also supplied to China. The *Romeo* Class proved popular with the Chinese and they commenced to produce them in Chinese yards at the rate of six per year. Of a slightly larger design, designated the Chinese *Romeo* Class, the first of these was launched in 1962.

In 1962 China produced her first ballistic missile firing submarine (SSB). Based on the Soviet *Golf* Class, it was conventionally powered and was fitted with two vertical missile launching tubes (the Soviet version had three tubes).

Between 1971 and 1981 a new class of submarines appeared. The *Ming* Class (SS) were Chinese-designed, but were heavily influenced by the *Romeo* Class.

The first Chinese nuclear powered submarines were the *Han* Class (SSN) of 5,550 tons submerged displacement, armed with six 21in torpedo tubes. A class of five, they were launched between 1971 and 1990. This class was followed by the much larger *Xia* Class Type 092 (SSBN) of 8,000 tones dived displacement. These are armed with Css-N3 SLBM, with a range of 1,460 NM, and six 21in torpedo tubes. The first of this class was launched in 1981 and the second in 1982, though one may have been lost in an accident. A new type of SSBN (Type 093) with a longer range missile is being developed. A class of four is envisaged to be launched by the year 2000. Four *Kilo* Class SSNs were ordered from Russia in 1993. The first arrived in China early in 1995 and a second followed in September the same year. Production of a new class of SSNs was commenced in late 1994 with Russian aid. This class is due to be launched between 1998 and 2001.

At the time of writing (1996) the Chinese submarine fleet consists of one SSBN (*Xia*), one SSB (*Golf*), two SSN (*Kilo*), five SSN (*Han*), one SSG (modified *Romeo*), ten SS (*Ming*) and thirty (plus thirty-five in reserve) SS (*Romeo*).

SUBMARINE INSIGNIA

The People's Liberation Army, of which the Navy is a component part, abolished all ranks and insignia on 1 June, 1965. At the same time the various branches of the PLA adopted a universal olive-drab uniform of austere appearance. Several years later the Naval and Air branches gradually incorporated more distinctive designs for their uniforms.

On 21 May, 1984, it was announced that new uniforms would be introduced and that proposals would be made to reintroduce ranks and rank insignia. The new uniforms for all three traditional services appeared in mid-1985 and the new rank insignia along with branch badges were authorized on 1 October, 1988.

By April, 1990, a submarine badge had made an appearance though its authenticity has, as yet, not been confirmed by official sources. It is said to be awarded to submarine commanders for superior performance. (The term 'commander', before rank titles was reintroduced, referred to all commissioned officers, so it is possible that other officers may qualify.) It is made of a dull gold-coloured metal and consists of the starboard bow view of a submarine within a wreath on the base of which is a tablet bearing the inscription 'HGTZH'. The whole is surmounted by a star, the centre of which encircles the Chinese inscription '8,1' (commemorating the date of the formation of the People's Liberation Army, 1 August, 1928). Representations of waves spread out from either side of the centre device.

The badge measures 60mm x 24mm and on the reverse are four Chinese characters, below which is the English inscription 'PPR Navy'. The insignia is normally fixed by two clutch fasteners, though other fixings are possible. It is presented in a box displaying two rows of Chinese characters.

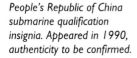

People's Republic of China submarine qualification insignia. Appeared in 1990, authenticity to be confirmed.

COLOMBIA

SUBMARINE SERVICE

The first Colombian submarines entered service in 1972. These were two midget SX-506 type submarines purchased in sections in Italy and transported to Colombia for assembly. Named *Intrepido* and *Indomable* they are of 58 tons surface displacement, 75.4 ft long and can carry eight attack swimmers with two tons of explosives as well as two SDVs (Swimmer Delivery Vehicles).

These were followed in 1975 by two 209 (type 1200) (SS) West German-built patrol submarines of 1,000 tons surface displacement and named *Pijao* and *Tayrona*. These four boats constitute the submarine force at the time of writing.

COLOMBIA

SUBMARINE INSIGNIA

The Colombian submarine badge, which is the same for all personnel, was instituted in 1973. It is made of metal with clutch fastenings and measures 70mm x 25mm. A cloth version is stamped on working overalls. The insignia is worn on all uniforms and is generally positioned on the left-hand-side breast pocket.

The insignia, which is coloured gold, depicts a 209 (type 1200) submarine in the centre of which is the Colombian Navy coat-of-arms in coloured enamel. Either side of the coat-of-arms is an inward-facing dolphin. A miniature version, 42mm x 14mm, also exists.

About 1991 a silver variation of the full-size badge appeared and was said to be for ratings. This has not been verified and it is quite possible that, like Spain and Chile, the insignia is for shore-based supporting personnel.

About the same date a new version of the standard insignia also put in an appearance. The two dolphins are replaced by two sharks which are situated entirely below the submarine, whereas the standard badge has their heads midway up the hull, also the naval coat-of-arms is replaced by the national coat-of-arms. It is possible that this may be a third variation

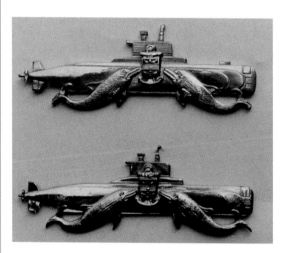

Colombian submarine qualification insignia, authorized 1973, showing slight variations in manufacture.

of the Amphibious Commando badge, the sharks being traditionally used on insignia by that unit. The first badge worn by the Amphibious Commandos depicted a gold or silver submarine below which were two sharks; behind the submarine was a parachute canopy. The second pattern showed a commando knife in place of the submarine with a full parachute overlaid by the navy coat-of-arms in the middle.

CROATIA

SUBMARINE SERVICE

The submarine service commenced about 1991 with the capture of the Yugoslav midget *Una* Class submarine 914. On incorporation into the Croatian Navy she was renamed *Soca*. Built in 1985 she displaced 86 tons surfaced. She can carry mines or six combat swimmers plus four swimmer delivery vehicles (SDV). In Croatian hands she was lengthened by twelve feet to incorporate a diesel engine. The construction of a 120 ton midget submarine to be armed with torpedo tubes and carrying SDVs is under consideration. There are also, in service, two former Yugoslav *Mala* Class SDVs.

SUBMARINE INSIGNIA

With such a small submarine force it is unlikely that any specialist insignia exists, though there may be an associated combat swimmers badge.

CUBA

SUBMARINE SERVICE

The Soviet Union transferred a *Foxtrot* Class submarine (SS) to Cuba in February, 1979. In May of the same year a Soviet *Whiskey* Class submarine (SS) was also transferred to Cuba. It became non-operational in 1987 and became a charging station and training facility.

A second *Foxtrot* was transferred to Cuba in January, 1980, and was followed by a third in February, 1984. These submarines are thought to be non-operational.

SUBMARINE INSIGNIA

It is unlikely that special submarine qualification badges exist at present.

DENMARK

SUBMARINE SERVICE

The submarine service was established in 1909 and the first Danish submarines were the eight boats of the *Havmanden* Class. These were Whitehead-built Holland type of Austrian design of which the first three were constructed in Italy in 1911 and the remainder in Denmark from 1911 to 1913. They had a surface displacement of 162 tons and were armed with two torpedo tubes. At the same time one Fiat *San Giorgio* type also entered service. This was a smaller boat of 105 tons surface displacement.

From 1912 to 1915 five *Aegir* (*Neptun*) Class Hay-Whitehead Holland type were constructed in Copenhagen. These boats had a surface displacement of 185 tons and were armed with three 18in torpedo tubes and one 1 pdr gun. They were followed in 1915/18 by three *Bellona* Class *Navy* type submarines of 301 tons surface displacement and armed with four torpedo tubes.

The *Daphne* Class of two boats was completed in 1925 and 1926. These had a surface displacement of 300 tons and were armed with six torpedo tubes and a 14 pdr AA gun.

By 1931 the service consisted of two *Daphne* Class, three *Bellona* Class, two *Aegir* Class and three *Havmanden* Class submarines. This was the force that was in being when Denmark was invaded by Germany in 1940. As a result of the invasion the Danish submarine service ceased to exist, all its boats being either scuttled or captured. After World War II the submarine branch was reconstituted with the transfer to Denmark of three ex-Royal Navy V Class submarines. They became UI (ex-Polish *Dzik*, ex-HMS/M P52), U2 (ex-HMS/M *Vulpine*) and U3 (ex-HMS/M *Morse*, ex-HMS/M *Vortex*) and remained in service until 1957, 1958 and 1968.

Between 1958 and 1964 four new submarines designated the *Delfinen* Class (SS) were constructed in Copenhagen. They had a surface displacement of 600 tons and were armed with four torpedo tubes. These were joined between 1968 and 1969 by two *Narhvalen* Class submarines (SSK) of the West German improved 205 Type built in Denmark under licence. They have a surface displacement of 370 tons and are armed with eight 21in torpedo tubes.

In 1987 Denmark purchased three German-built Type 207 *Kobben* Class submarines (SSK) from Norway. Modernization, including lengthening, commenced the same year.

By 1990 the *Delfinen* Class had been withdrawn from service leaving only the two *Narhvalen* Class and the three *Tumleren* Class (ex-*Kobben*) in service.

SUBMARINE INSIGNIA

The first distinctive submarine badge actually worn was an unofficial one designed in 1972 by Lieutenant-Commander P. B. Soerensen. This came after a period of general discontentment in the submarine service, mainly over pay and career prospects. During this period repeated requests for a special insignia were turned down. The general idea was to keep the uniform free from the multiplicity of insignia worn by some other navies.

This unauthorized insignia was manufactured in gold and red embroidery on dark blue cloth. It consisted of a fouled encircled anchor surmounted by a crown and with a dolphin on each side. It measured 84mm by 41mm and was worn sewn onto the right breast. Sixty badges were made and were worn, as a protest, by all officers in the submarine squadron. The Naval Command reacted quickly and an official badge was authorized in less than a year.

At the same time as this unofficial embroidered badge an unofficial home-made metal badge was quite popular among submarine crews. It was made in quantity by submarine engineering personnel and showed a *Delfinen* Class submarine cut from an aluminium ring. This ring is the component left behind when a submarine signal is fired through an ejector. It was then mounted on the back part of a navy button and worn on the working rig.

The official insignia was approved by the Chief of the Navy on 12 October, 1973, and was authorized for wear from 25 April, 1974. The insignia is made in gold thread embroidery on dark blue fabric. It shows a fouled anchor under a crown with a leaping dolphin on either side. The dimensions are 50mm wide by 50mm high. There is only one grade and size and the same insignia is worn by both officers and ratings.

The insignia is worn by personnel attached to the Submarine Squadron who have passed their submarine training and have served in submarines for five months. Personnel with at least three years' service in submarines are entitled to wear the insignia in perpetuity.

The insignia is worn sewn onto the right side of the uniform in such a way that a horizontal line through the centre of the device would be level with the top of the breast pocket.

A gilt metal badge was produced at the beginning of 1989 measuring 47mm x 44mm with a brooch fastening. The original design was not popular mainly due to the shape of the dolphins. A second more pleasing version was produced in August, 1989, and, though still not official, it is universally worn on shirts and sweaters.

A cloth insignia can be worn on the upper right arm of the sweater. It consists of a disc 87mm in diameter with the Danish word for Submarine at the top and the abbreviation for Squadron at the bottom. The central device is the crest of the Submarine Squadron. The cap ribbons of ratings serving in submarines bear the word 'UNDERVANDSBÅD' meaning submarine.

Danish unofficial submarine qualification insignia worn by officers 1972-3.

Danish official submarine qualification insignia, all ranks, authorized 25 April, 1974.

Danish submarine identification badge worn on the right sleeve of the sweater.

Danish submarine qualification insignia in metal.
Left: first type (January, 1989) with dolphins' fins above anchor flukes.
Right: second type (August, 1989) with dolphins' fins touching anchor flukes.

ECUADOR

SUBMARINE SERVICE

The Submarine Branch of the Ecuadorian Navy was established in 1974 with the commissioning of the West German-built type 209 patrol submarine (SSK) *Shyri*. A second type 209, the *Huancavilca*, was commissioned in 1987. They have a surface displacement of 980 tons and are armed with eight 21in torpedo tubes. These two boats constitute the present Ecuadorian Navy Submarine Squadron.

SUBMARINE INSIGNIA

The submarine insignia was authorized in June, 1974. It is the same for all rank grades. The insignia is manufactured in metal and consists of a type 209 submarine with a central device, in silver of an eagle encircled by a rope all superimposed on a wreath. It faces the wearer's left. Early badges were of bronze metal and lacked a schnorkel on the sail. Stars may be added to the ballast tank to the right of the eagle device. One silver star represents one patrol of forty-five days duration and one gold star replaces three silver stars. The insignia comes in two sizes. The standard device measures 70mm x 20mm and the smaller one, for wear on mess dress, is about half the size. Fixings consist of brooch, clutch and screw fastenings and the insignia is worn on the right-hand pocket of jackets and shirts.

Qualification for the badge consists of successfully completing the basic submarine course, of one and a half years, within Ecuador or elsewhere.

Ecuadorian submarine qualification insignia with one patrol star.

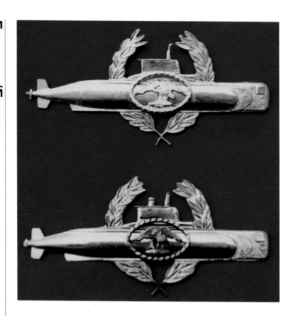

Ecuadorian submarine qualification insignia. Top first type 1974 with periscope only, bottom second type with 'snort' added 1980.

EGYPT

SUBMARINE SERVICE

The Egyptian Navy first included submarines in its order-of-battle in 1957. Between that year and 1969 the Soviet Union transferred nine *Whiskey* class submarines (SS) and three MV class small coastal submarines (SS) to Egypt. The latter only remained in service for a short period.

Eight Soviet *Romeo* Class submarines (SS) were transferred between 1966 and 1969, during which time two of the *Whiskeys* were returned to the USSR.

By the mid-1970s the submarine flotilla consisted of six *Romeos* and six *Whiskeys*. The mid-1980s saw the deletion of two of the *Romeos* but these were replaced by four Chinese-built *Romeos*. The remaining *Whiskeys* were also subsequently deleted. In 1994 approval was given for the USA to fund the construction, in Germany, of two Type 209 Class submarines (SSK) to be fitted with US equipment. These are not likely to enter service much before the end of the century.

The present (1996) submarine force consists of two ex-Soviet *Romeos* and four ex-Chinese *Romeos*. There are also several Italian-designed two-man SDVs.

Submarine Insignia

Little information is available on the Egyptian submarine insignia. Most likely it was authorized in the early 1960s. The badge comes in two sizes, 83mm x 24mm for submarine commanders and a smaller version 55mm x 16mm for submarine officers. They are variously described as being manufactured in gold plate, gilt or bronze metal but most appear to be stamped in brass. The insignia comprises a submarine, facing to the wearer's left, with the national Falcon device in the centre. They are fixed to the uniform with brooch fasteners. The original design varied from the present one in that the conning tower was less streamlined and it was said that they were hand-stamped in the Egyptian Naval Dockyard.

Two other badges, that cannot be verified, are said to exist. One for senior ratings similar to the officer's badge but mounted on a brass ring approximately 50mm in diameter, and one for ratings, possibly in silver or white metal, measuring 45mm x 12mm but without the ring.

A further design exists. This depicts a simple submarine facing the wearer's left. The hull is ornamented by a series of six ovals, then three Arabic characters followed by a further three ovals. It measures 81mm x 20mm (though this can vary) and is made in gold plate, polished brass or casting metal. The quality varies considerably. It is also produced mounted on a 52mm diameter brass ring. Some of these are made in Egyptian bazaars and others are made by an Egyptian company in Canada who claimed that they would gain official approval in 1989. Egyptian Naval Authorities are adamant that these are bogus and certainly unofficial.

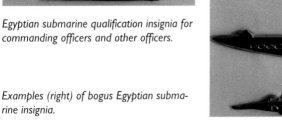

Egyptian submarine qualification insignia for commanding officers and other officers.

Examples (right) of bogus Egyptian submarine insignia.

ESTONIA

SUBMARINE SERVICE

Estonia's submarine service was short-lived. Two submarine minelayers were constructed in Great Britain for Estonia and entered service as the *Kalev* and *Lembit* in 1937. They had a surface displacement of 620 tons and were armed with four 21in torpedo tubes and a single 4in AA gun. The mine-laying capacity consisted of twenty mines. Both boats were seized by the Soviet Union on 17 June, 1940, and were incorporated into the Soviet Navy.

SUBMARINE INSIGNIA

It is unlikely that any special submarine insignia ever existed.

FINLAND

SUBMARINE SERVICE

Finland's first submarine was a Holland Class ex-Russian boat, the AG16. It had been scuttled by its Russian crew on 3 April, 1918, at Hango, then raised by Finland in 1924. It was never repaired and was eventually broken up in 1929.

In the years 1926 and 1927 three submarines were laid down in Finnish shipyards. These were commissioned between 1924 and 1931 as the *Vetehinen*, *Vesihiisi* and *Ikuturso*. They had a surface displacement of 493 tons and were armed with four 21in torpedo tubes, one 76mm gun and one 20mm machine gun.

A fourth submarine, the *Saukko*, was laid down in 1929 and commissioned in 1931. A tiny boat, she displaced just 90 tons and was armed with two 18in torpedo tubes and a 13mm gun.

In 1933 a fifth submarine was launched. She was funded by the German Government to carry out trials and to act as a prototype at a time when such activity was prohibited by the Versailles Treaty. In 1934 she was taken over by the Finnish Navy and named *Vesikko*. She had a surface displacement of 250 tons and was armed with three 21in torpedo tubes.

All five submarines survived the Winter War and the Continuation War (World War II) and were credited with sinking at least four Soviet submarines. At the end of the war they were disarmed by the Allied Supervisory Committee.

The Treaty of Paris in 1947 prohibited Finland from having submarines. All but the *Vesikko* were sold to Belgium in 1953 for scrap. The *Vesikko* was preserved in the hope that the Navy would be allowed to keep one submarine for A/S training purposes. This was not allowed. In 1959 she was transferred to the Military Museum of Finland at Helsinki and opened to the public in 1973.

Submarine Insignia
It is unlikely that any special submarine insignia ever existed.

FRANCE

Submarine Service
France was the first country to adopt the submarine as a vessel of war. The honour of being the world's first offensive submarine went to the *Gymnôte*, a boat of 30 tons displacement armed with two torpedos carried in slings. She was launched in 1888 and a year later she was followed by the *Gustave Zédé*. This second submarine was considerably larger, displacing 270 tons, and was armed with one torpedo tube. The *Morse*, of 146 tons displacement, followed in 1899. All three were extremely successful. Numerous similar boats followed.

Seventeen classes were constructed before World War I. At the commencement of hostilities France had ninety-two submarines. At the war's end sixty-two submarines remained in service. After peace was declared, forty-six ex-German U-Boats were ceded to France of which ten were incorporated into the French Navy.

Between the wars, as an economical alternative to battleships and for mercantile warfare, France built up a sizable submarine fleet. Among these vessels was, perhaps, the world's most famous submarine, the *Surcouf*. Classed as a submarine cruiser, she displaced 2,880 tons and was armed with two 8in guns, eight 21.7in torpedo tubes, four 15.7in torpedo tubes, two 37mm AA guns and two 13.2mm AA guns. In addition she carried a sea-plane, only the fifth submarine in the world to do so. She was designed for extended operations against trade and could cruise unreplenished for ninety days. A boarding launch was carried and there was a compartment sufficiently large to hold forty prisoners-of-war.

At the outbreak of World War II France had just under one hundred submarines in service. However, by the Fall of France the great majority were either sunk, scuttled or interned. Fifteen submarines escaped to join the Fighting French, including the *Surcouf*. Five were eventually lost, one of which was the *Surcouf*, lost in a collision in 1942. A further two were scrapped before the war's end. The Free French Flotilla was augmented by the transfer of three ex-Royal Navy U/V Class submarines and one ex-Italian boat.

The reconstituted French Navy started its peacetime service with thirty-six submarines, the majority of which had spent the war years interned. This number was increased by the acquisition of five ex-German U-Boats.

Post-war submarine construction commenced with the 1,320 ton *Narval* Class (SS) of six vessels and the smaller 400 ton *Aretuse* Class (SS) of four vessels, all of which were launched between 1957 and 1960. These were followed by the highly successful *Daphne* Class (SSK) of 860 tons surface displacement. Ten of this class were constructed for the French Navy of which the *Eurydice* was lost and *Sirene* was sunk but later recovered and returned to service. Further boats were built for export.

In 1964 a conventionally powered experimental submarine of 3,000 tons, the *Gymnôte*, was launched. She was armed with two missile launching tubes and her role was to carry out trials for the firing of ICBMs for France's future deterrent force.

The first nuclear propelled submarine was *Redoutable*, the name-ship of her class (SSBN). She had a surface displacement of 8,080 tons and carried sixteen ballistic missiles plus four 21in torpedo tubes. Five sister submarines were added between 1973 and 1985. The lead ship was paid off in December, 1991, and the class was re-named *L'Inflexible*.

Perhaps the last conventionally powered French submarines, the four 1,200 ton *Agosta* Class (SSK), entered service between 1977 and 1978. Equally successful to the *Daphne* Class, they also led to foreign orders.

France's first nuclear-powered hunter-killer submarine (SSN) made its appearance in 1979 with the launching of the 2,385 ton displacement *Rubis*, the name-ship of its class. She commissioned in February, 1983, and five further vessels commissioned between 1984 and 1993. Boats of the *Rubis* Class are armed with four 21in torpedo tubes and are capable of firing missiles.

A follow-on class of three, possibly four, SSBNs to the *L'Inflexible* Class are the *Le Triomphant* Class. The name-ship will be commissioned in September, 1996, and the remainder should be in service by 2005. These large submarines will have a surface displacement of 12,640 tons and will be armed with sixteen SLBM of an advanced nature. At the time of writing (1996) the French Submarine Force consists of five *L'Inflexible* Class (SSBN) '*Le Force de Dissuasion*', six *Rubis* Class (SSN), four *Agosta* Class (SSK) and three *Daphne* Class (SSK).

Submarine Insignia

Before the approval of a special submarine qualification badge for all ranks, submarine service ratings, from the early 1930s, wore a distinctive cloth branch badge on their upper left sleeve. The device consisted of crossed torpedoes with six bolts of lightning radiating outwards. It was worn in gold, yellow or red on blue, depending on rank, and measured 70mm wide.

On 24 December, 1946, a metal badge for all qualified submarine personnel was created. This depicted a gold-coloured *Narval* class submarine in its original configuration with a stepped sail (conning tower) facing its wearer's left. This was superimposed on a white metal compass rose in the form of a ring with an upright white metal sword with a gold hilt (behind the submarine) in the centre. It measured 55m x 48mm and was secured by clutch fasteners. A cloth version in red or yellow embroidery was phased out in the mid-1950s. (On 16 August, 1961, this badge was redesigned as a superior grade insignia intended primarily for officers and certain senior ratings with special qualifications.) At the same time a second badge, designated as an elementary grade insignia, was authorized mainly for junior ratings and later for certain other categories pending qualification for the superior insignia. Its design consisted of the same gold-coloured submarine, but mounted on a smaller diameter compass rose and bearing the cardinal points only. This also lacked the vertical sword. It measured 55mm x 30mm. This was phased out in 1967. From 1961 to 1967 the superior grade insignia was restricted to officers who had been in command for two years and other officers with four years of submarine service.

The system was changed with the implementation of three grades on 16 December, 1974. The new badges are much like their two predecessors but the sail (conning tower) of the submarine is streamlined. The lowest grade is issued to officers who hold a certificate of general knowledge in submarines and to ratings with an elementary submarine certificate. It is similar in design to the original superior badge but lacks the vertical sword and is known as 'without swords'. The next grade is issued to officers who are qualified in submarine navigation, or as seamen or engineer watch officers of a nuclear submarine or who hold a superior submarine certificate. For ratings it is granted to those who hold a submarine certificate of the higher grade. The design is almost identical to

FRANCE

the previous superior badge. It is known as 'with one sword'. The highest grade is worn by commanding officers and former commanding officers only. It is known as 'with two swords criss-crossed'. All three badges measure 55mm x 48mm and have clutch fastenings.

The submarine badges are worn on uniform in one size only, though a smaller version, 19mm x 16mm is available for wear on civilian clothes. The insignia can be worn throughout the recipient's service but it can be withdrawn for disciplinary reasons.

A new version (its authenticity has yet to be verified) was introduced about 1989. This bears the 1974 submarine design mounted on a simple

French submarine crew branch badge pre-1946. Gold wire embroidery optional for senior ratings otherwise yellow embroidery. Not worn by officers.

French submarine crew branch badge pre-1946. Red embroidery for junior ratings. These badges were replaced in 1946 by the new metal insignia, though junior ratings at first wore the new design in red embroidery on cloth.

French submarine qualification insignia 1946 to 1974.
Top: elementary qualification.
Bottom: superior qualification.

silver-coloured ring 25mm in diameter. This may be for shore based support personnel.

The official description of how insignia is to be worn is as follows, 'worn on the right-hand side of the chest on all dress uniforms where decorative ribbons are allowed. The insignia is placed in the middle of the chest pocket on all white and khaki jackets and shirts, and above the pleat on the chest of the blue jacket'.

Sailors serving in submarines wear on their cap tallies the words 'SOUS-MARIN' followed by the submarine's name.

French submarine qualification insignia 'without swords' 1974.

French submarine qualification insignia 'with one sword' 1974.

French submarine qualification insignia 'with two swords' 1974.

French submarine insignia about 1990, possibly shore support, elementary, or maybe unofficial.

GERMANY: EMPIRE

SUBMARINE SERVICE

Uncertain as to the value of the submarine as a tool of war, Germany was a late starter in this field. Using the knowledge gained by other nations her first boats, when they did appear, were right up-to-date. The first boat, the U-1, was launched on 30 August 1905 (though two experimental boats had been launched in 1890 but were never actively employed).

U-1 was very successful and was roughly equivalent to the British D Class. She had a displacement of 197 tons and was armed with one bow torpedo tube and three 17.7in torpedoes were carried. A further twenty-nine boats in five classes were completed so that Germany commenced World War I with thirty submarines in service of which twenty were operational. These, unlike the Royal Navy's submarines, were all in home waters based at Kiel, Wilhelmshaven and Heligoland.

Being a military power, Germany initially did not appreciate the value of the submarine. It was not until stalemate on the Western Front that submarine warfare was stepped up. Once the U-boat's value was appreciated the U-boat arm was given priority. It was a very efficient organization and its personnel were well trained. Their average diving time was a remarkable twenty-seven seconds. By 1917 seventy-two submarines had been constructed.

Wartime construction was based on nine main classes including: ocean going, coastal, mine-laying and merchant types. By the war's end 345 had been built. Some mounted 5.9in guns and U-12 made history on 1 January, 1915, when she operated a small aircraft from her foredeck.

German submarines sank nearly 12 million tons of Allied shipping in World War I but lost 178 U-boats and 5,364 out of the 13,000 officers and men in the U-boat arm. After the armistice the U-boat arm was either interned or scuttled. Two hundred and three boats surrendered; all, with the exception of ten ex-French boats, were scrapped between 1922 and 1923.

SUBMARINE INSIGNIA

On 1 February, 1918, by order of the Kaiser, submariners of the Imperial German Navy were authorized to wear a distinctive insignia. It was manufactured in heavy gold-coloured metal 48mm x 46mm. The design consisted of a U-boat facing the wearer's left completely surrounded by a wreath. The official description stated that the composition of the upper half of the wreath was to be of laurel leaves and the lower half was to be of oak leaves. However, only laurel leaves actually appear on the badge. The leaves of the wreath were bound together by a representation of a ribbon. The entire device was surmounted by an Imperial Crown. On the reverse was a substantial vertical hinged securing pin and hook and the name of the manufacturer, Zeither-Berlin, was inscribed on the back of the submarine.

The same design was worn by all ranks on the lower part of the left breast. Unlike the submarine insignia of most other countries which were for professional qualifications, the German insignia was regarded more as a reward for war service. An unofficial miniature (34mm x 29mm) appeared some years after World War I.

U-boat crews were distinguished by their cap ribbons which bore the words 'UNTERSEEBOOT' or 'U-BOOT' in conjunction with the number of their flotilla, half flotilla, base or function. All tallies were in capital letters during World War I, changed to lower case in World War II.

German Submarine War Badge 1918.

GERMANY: 1918-45

SUBMARINE SERVICE

The Treaty of Versailles forbade Germany from having submarines. However, in order to gain experience for the future, the German Government financed the construction of two submarines in the Netherlands for the Turkish Navy. Later this method was again used to supply five submarines to Finland, one to Spain and a further one to Turkey. When the Treaty was finally abrogated, the U-boat arm was one of the first units to be re-established.

GERMANY

The first post-war submarines, three in number, were commissioned in 1936. They displaced 862 tons, mounted two 5.9in guns and carried six 19.7in torpedo tubes. These were quickly followed by five more classes totalling fifty-eight boats.

At the commencement of war in 1939 Germany had fifty-seven U-boats in commission. A massive production programme then began. It consisted of five main types: cruiser, ocean-going, sea-going, coastal and mine-laying submarines. In all 1,074 submarines were completed. Perhaps the two most potent developments were the schnorkel (originally a Dutch invention) and the acoustic homing torpedo (Gnat).

Germany's U-boat arm very nearly changed the course of the war. As a measure of its success, at the peak of the Battle of the Atlantic, in June, 1943, it sank nearly 650,000 tons of Allied shipping. The total tonnage destroyed during the war amounted to 14.5 million tons.

At the end of the war, of the 1,162 U-boats in operational service, it is generally accepted that 784 were lost, 157 surrendered and 221 were scuttled. Of the 39,000 U-boat officers and men only 7,000 survived. Germany was again without a submarine fleet.

(As there is a vast literary coverage of the Kriegsmarine U-boat arm — probably more than any other similar force — this section has been deliberately abbreviated and only the salient details have been mentioned.)

SUBMARINE INSIGNIA 1939-45

Following the Kaiser's example Hitler authorized a submarine war badge (*U-Boot Kriegsabzeichen*) on 13 October, 1939. Like its predecessor it was more of an award than a qualification. It was awarded to submariners after two sorties against the enemy. However, an immediate award could be made to individuals who won a bravery decoration, were wounded or who had been involved in a particularly successful mission. The insignia, which was manufactured in heavy-gold coloured metal, showed a submarine facing the wearer's right surmounted by an eagle and swastika. Behind the eagle's wings and surrounding the submarine was a laurel wreath tied together at the base by a crossed ribbon. The badge measured 48mm x 39mm.

The insignia was produced in various standards of quality and with minor differences in design. The insignias made early in the war were of a very fine quality but the workmanship of later models, some of which were made in France, could not compare. The early badges displayed the manufacturer's name on the reverse (Schwerin und Sohn, Berlin) and were secured by a broad vertical hinged pin and hook. The later models showed the manufacturer's initials only, eg FO (for Frederich Orth), and had a narrow pin and hook fastener. Later patterns made in France had horizontal pins. There was also a cloth version, gilt wire on silk for officers and gold cloth on felt for ratings.

A special insignia was presented to particularly successful U-Boat commanders who had first to be holders of the Knight's Cross of the Iron Cross with oak leaves. It was of the same standard design but was manufactured in silver and had nine diamonds inset on the swastika.

Grossadmiral Karl Dönitz was presented with a unique insignia produced in gold with twenty-one diamonds on the swastika and a further twelve on the wreath.

On 26 July, 1957, the submarine war badge was de-nazified by the removal of the eagle and swastika. It also appears in miniature with a black Maltese Cross in place of the eagle and swastika. This style was worn by submarine old comrades organizations. Like other de-nazified insignia it was, in 1957, miniaturized in silver and worn on uniforms attached to a small black ribbon 30mm wide and worn in conjunction with medal ribbons.

U-Boat crew could also be distinguished by their cap ribbons which bore the words, in gothic lettering, 'Unterseebootsflottille' followed by the flotilla name. Unofficial badges were often worn on the sides of caps by individual U-Boat crews. There were numerous designs such as sharks, weapons and flowers. They were not allowed to be worn ashore. U-Boat Captains were distinguished at sea by wearing white cap covers.

To bring awards to U-Boat crews in line with awards available to the Army and Air Force, submarine combat clasps (*U-Boat Frontspange*) were introduced in 1944. The insignia was created in bronze metal on 15 May and in silver metal on the 24 November. Later in the war a gilt or gold badge was authorized but it is unlikely that it was ever awarded.

The U-Boat combat clasp depicted a central device similar to the submarine war badge, the only differences being that the wings of the eagle followed the curvature of the wreath and the crossed ribbon at the base was replaced by crossed swords. On either side was a spray of six oak leaves. The reverse had a large horizontal hinged pin and hook fastener and bore the manufacturer's mark and the name of the designer, 'PEEKHAUS'. For exceptional U-Boat Commanders the badge was awarded with diamonds. It measured 74mm x 24mm. The U-Boat combat clasps were awarded for continuous service in action, gallantry and tenacious conduct on active service. The various grades indicated ascending achievements. On 26 July, 1957, the insignia was de-nazified by the removal of the eagle and swastika. This altered device measured 77mm

GERMANY

x 24mm and like the submarine war badge was miniaturized and worn on a black ribbon 30mm wide.

Though not primarily a submarine award, the combat badge for small fighting units (*Kampfabzeichen der Kleinkampfmittel*, otherwise 'K' men or frogmen) is included because the insignia was also awarded to crews of miniature submarines. The award was created on 30 November, 1944, and came in seven classes, the first four of which were cloth and the remainder in metal (though cloth versions of these were also produced). The four cloth insignias were of yellow or gold embroidery on a navy blue disc 80mm in diameter. The basic design consisted of a leaping swordfish (or sawfish) behind which was a circle of rope knotted at the top. The first (or basic) class displayed the swordfish and rope only and was awarded for two months' service in which a mission was planned and achieved good results. The second class displayed a single sword on a forty-five degree angle pointed to the wearer's right behind the basic design. It was awarded for one combat action. The third class displayed two crossed swords behind the basic device and was awarded for two combat actions. The fourth class displayed three swords behind the basic device and was awarded for three or four combat actions.

The three senior awards in metal consisted of a leaping swordfish superimposed on a loosely coiled and knotted rope, measuring 70mm x 22mm and secured by a horizontal pin and hook on the reverse. The bronze or fifth class was awarded for five or six combat actions. The silver or sixth class was awarded for seven, eight or nine combat actions and the gold or seventh class was awarded for ten or more combat actions. Little evidence exists as to whether these badges were ever actually worn in wartime, though, as they contained no nazi emblems, they were reintroduced by the Bundesmarine as commemorative awards in 1957.

Though not a submarine qualification badge, a bronze insignia was presented to dockyard employees working on U-Boats. It depicted a U-Boat facing the wearer's right with a cogged wheel encircling its middle section and surmounted by the German Eagle and swastika. It measured 33mm x 23mm and was fixed to clothing by a 49mm stick pin. Its German name was *Werftleistungsabzeichen*.

There are several types of U-Boat old comrade badges dating from about 1957. Most depict miniature, de-nazified versions of the U-Boat War Badge or U-Boat Combat Clasp in gold, silver or bronze. Numerous other unofficial badges connected with the U-Boat service abound. Most are connected with specific units. An insignia resembling an oval breast badge was said to have been worn by recruits on completion of their training and awaiting assignment to a U-Boat. This was of course quite unofficial. It consisted of a diving submarine below the inscription '*frontreif*' ('ripe for the front') surrounded by a German Eagle and swastika. It was secured by a vertical flat brooch pin and clasp and was made in either brass or grey metal.

German Submarine War Service Badge 1939-45.

German Submarine War Service Badges 1939-45, de-Nazified 1957. (50mm x 37mm).

German Submarine War Service Badge 1939-45, de-Nazified for Submarine Old Comrades Association.

German Submarine Combat Clasp (Frontspange) bronze, 15 May 1944.

German Submarine Combat Clasp (Frontspange) silver, 24 November 1944.

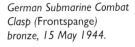

GERMANY

German Submarine Combat
Clasp (Frontspange),
1944-5, de-Nazified 1957.

German Small Fighting Units (Kampfabzeichen der Kleinkampfmittel) insignia 1944.
In yellow embroidery on black cloth for junior grades. Left: 1st grade, right: 2nd grade.

German Small Fighting Units (Kampfabzeichen der Kleinkampfmittel) insignia 1944.
Left: 3rd grade, right: 4th grade.

*German Small Fighting Units (*Kampfabzeichen der Klein-kampfmittel*) insignia 1944. In metal for three senior grades. 5th grade bronze, 6th grade silver, 7th grade gold.*

German lapel badge for civilian dockyard employees working on U-Boats, 1944-5.

GERMANY: FEDERAL REPUBLIC

SUBMARINE SERVICE

After gaining full independence in 1955 West Germany was allowed to build up a naval force. The first submarines entered Bundesmarine service in 1956. There were three re-built former wartime U-Boats, two of the XXIII Type and one of the XXI Type. They were followed by two classes of small coastal submarines, eleven 419 ton Type 205 (SS) from 1961 to 1969 and eighteen 450 ton Type 206 (SSK) from 1973 to 1975.

A further class of four vessels designated the Type 212 (SSK) is projected to enter service by 2003. These boats will have a surface displacement of 1,320 tons and will be armed with six 21in torpedo tubes. They will also have a minelaying capacity.

At the time of writing (1996) the German submarine force numbers six Type 206 and twelve Type 206A (modified Type 206). These are supported by two type 205, relegated for trails and target duties.

SUBMARINE INSIGNIA

The first appearance of a submarine badge was about 1965. This was the Submarine Specialist Qualification, awarded to ratings on completion of training at the Basic Submarine Training School (Gesubtng), Neustadt. Made of cloth, it depicted, on a disc of 50mm diameter, an embroidered submarine of basic design facing the wearer's right above two rows of waves. It was worn on the left sleeve just above the cuff and was manufactured in red on blue and red on white (gold and yellow versions on blue and white were worn by senior ratings). This insignia which first appeared in the 1968 Dress Regulations became obsolete in 1982. From 1972 to 1982 it was worn by ratings who did not qualify for the later breast insignia described below.

In June, 1972, a new submarine qualification badge was authorized. The first dress regulations illustrating this badge appeared on 16 March, 1982, some ten years later. It was to be awarded to all ranks after six months' service on board a submarine plus successfully completing submarine training. The insignia was manufactured in cloth and showed a submarine design facing the wearer's left, behind which was a simple oak leaf wreath. The device was to be worn on the right upper breast. It was manufactured in deep yellow on dark blue, but officers, at their own discretion, could wear it in gold wire embroidery. For other types of uniform it also came in yellow on olive drab and yellow or gold on white. The standard measurement was 78mm x 33mm but some were produced in widths of 80, 83 and 84mm. By mid-1988 it was generally felt that these badges were too big so they were all reduced to 64mm x 28mm.

A gold-coloured metal version of the cloth badge appeared some time before 1984. It was quite unofficial but was universally worn on shirts. It depicted a more stylized submarine resembling the 206 Class and on the back it bore the inscription 'NAVY-YACHT-SERVICE 04421/203090'. It was fixed to the shirt by horizontal brooch type pin and it measured 59mm x 35mm. A miniature was also produced measuring 30mm x 24mm on a vertical stick pin. In 1990 this unofficial metal insignia was upgraded to a more detailed design. The backs either bore the inscription 'DEUMER Ludenscheid' or were plain. This model measured 63mm x 35mm but several hand-made variations appeared, mostly measuring 77mm x 35mm. Occasionally these badges are worn on leather thongs incorporating a button hole for suspension of the insignia from buttons on certain types of uniforms.

In mid-1987 an official gold-coloured metal badge was authorized for wear on shirts and sweaters. It consisted of a submarine of the same design as the earlier cloth insignia but embossed on a curved and contoured pebbled plate measuring 75mm x 25mm. Two clutch fasteners were provided for fixing the insignia to clothing. It was awarded for six months' service on board a submarine, a somewhat lesser qualification than that stated for the cloth badge. It has not proved popular and many submariners continue to wear the unofficial versions.

Cap ribbons further distinguish submarine ratings by the inclusion of the word 'UNTERSEEBOOT'. This has now largely lapsed as, since 1974, the lowest submarine rank is Petty Officer.

German first post-war submarine badge, about 1965 to 1972. Specialist qualification awarded to ratings on completion of training at the Basic Submarine School (Gesubtng) Neustadt. It was worn on the left sleeve just above the cuff.

German submarine qualification insignia, yellow on dark blue, worn in winter by all ranks after six months on board a submarine plus successful completion of submarine training. Worn from June ,1972. (80mm).

German submarine qualification insignia, as above but yellow on white. (84mm).

German submarine qualification insignia, as previous example but yellow on olive drab for working uniform. (84mm).

German submarine
qualification insignia
embroidered in gold wire.
Worn by officers and
warrant officers at their
discretion. Various sizes.

German official metal
submarine qualification
insignia produced mid-
1987. Though the only
official metal submarine
badge it is seldom worn.
Most personnel favour the
unofficial styles.

German unofficial metal
submarine qualification
insignia, first design 1984.
Depicts a Type 206
submarine. Inscription on
reverse is 'Navy-Yacht-
Service 04421/203090'.

German unofficial metal submarine qualification insignia, second design 1990. Depicts a Type 206 submarine as before, but has more detail. Inscription on reverse is 'DEUMER Ludenscheid' or left plain.

GERMANY/GREECE

GREECE

SUBMARINE SERVICE

Greece first showed interest in submarines when in 1886 she purchased a Nordenfelt I, the first type to be armed with a torpedo. Used for experimental purposes, it is doubtful if she every entered active Naval service. The first submarines to join the fleet were two French-built Laubeuf type, the *Delphin* and the *Xiphias*. Completed in 1911 and 1912 they displaced 295 tons and were armed with five torpedo tubes. Both were seized by the French in December, 1916, and incorporated into the French Navy, only to be returned in 1917.

The next submarines to enter Greek service were two Schneider Laubeuf type, again French-built. They displaced 576 tons and were armed with four 21in torpedo tubes, one 4in gun and one 3 pdr AA gun. Named *Katsonis* and *Papmicolis* they were commissioned in 1927. Within a year four more submarines were completed in France for the Greek Navy. They were designated the *Glavkos* Class and named *Nereus, Proteus, Triton* and *Glavkos*. They displaced 700 tons and were armed with eight 21in torpedo tubes, one 4in gun and a 3 pdr AA gun. Three of these boats were later to be lost in World War II.

During the invasion of Greece in 1940 five submarines escaped to serve under Allied operational control. Between 1943 and 1946 the Royal Navy loaned six submarines to the Greek Navy, one P Class and five U/V Class. All were returned by 1956. In addition to these one Italian submarine was taken over in 1943 and continued in service until 1954.

The United States loaned the post-war Greek Navy two ex-*Gato* Class submarines (SS) in 1957. One was returned in 1967 and the other returned in 1972. In addition an ex-*Balao* Class (SS) was loaned in 1965 and purchased in 1976.

The first modern submarines, purposely built for Greece, were four 209 Class (type 1100) (SSK) constructed in West Germany. They displaced 1,100 tons and were armed with eight 21in torpedo tubes. They entered service between 1971 and 1973 as the *Glavkos* Class. These were followed by the acquisition of two more ex-USN submarines, a *Guppy* IIA (SS) in 1972 and a *Guppy* III (SS) in 1973. West Germany supplied a further four submarines of the 209 Class (type 1200) (SSK) between 1979 and 1980. Similar in most respects to the previously delivered 209s, they were incorporated into the same class. Both *Guppies* were deleted in 1993.

At the time of writing (1996) the submarine arm consists of eight *Glavros* Class type 209 Class (SSK).

SUBMARINE INSIGNIA

The Greek submarine insignia was first authorized in 1916. The badge in current use is made of gold coloured metal, for officers and petty officers, and measures 65mm x 10mm. For junior ratings it is made in silver-coloured metal and measures 45mm x 10mm. The design is the same for all ranks and consists of a British Type U/V Class submarine facing the wearer's right. Both types can be fixed to clothing by clutch or screw fasteners. An embroidered gold wire insignia is available to officers and petty officers at their own discretion as is a miniature badge for mess dress.

The insignia is worn on the upper part of the left breast above decorations. In order to qualify personnel must successfully complete the submarine school course. For Officers the course lasts five months, for senior Petty Officers three to five months and for junior ratings two to three months.

Until 1970 submarine badges were hand-made by Naval technicians. Because of this slight variation occurred in their manufacture. They are now produced commercially being cast/pressed and follow a uniform pattern.

About 1957 an unofficial design appeared in the shape of foreshortened *Gato* Class (ex-US) submarine. It was made of highly polished flat .032in thick brass, faced its' wearer's right and was fixed by two clutch fasteners. Its dimensions were 60mm x 22mm. There is also an unofficial velcro-backed cloth badge.

Sailors serving in submarines wear a cap tally prefixed with the letters 'Y/B', meaning submarine, followed by the boat's name eg 'Y/B Τριτον' (submarine Triton). By 1988 few junior ratings were employed in submarines; the smaller silver badge has therefore been withdrawn from issue and the submarine cap tallies are seldom seen.

The Greek Royal Navy Campaign Cross (ribbon equal widths of blue, white, blue) was instituted on 22 December, 1943, and awarded for at least six months' active and meritorious service at sea during World War II. It was awarded for those serving in submarines for more than a year and taking part in at least three patrols. On service dress when only ribbons were worn an additional black ribbon 37mm wide was worn. On this, in the form of metal clasps, were fixed miniature submarines, gold for officers, silver for petty officers and bronze for junior ratings.

Greek submarine qualification insignia. Top: in gold-coloured metal (65mm) for officers and senior ratings. Bottom in silver-coloured metal (44mm) for junior ratings. Design based on original hand-made badges (1916) but from 1970 professionally manufactured.

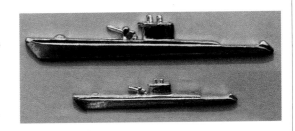

Greek submarine qualification insignia in gold wire embroidery for officers.

Devices worn on the Greek Royal Navy Campaign Cross 1943 for six months' active or meritorious service at sea World War II. Gold for officers, silver for senior ratings and bronze for junior ratings.

Greek unofficial submarine insignia worn from about 1957 to 1972 in Gato Class submarines on loan from the United States.

INDIA

SUBMARINE SERVICE

India took delivery of its first submarines between 1968 and 1969 with the arrival of three newly constructed Soviet *Foxtrot*s (SS). Five more followed between 1970 and 1975.

In 1986 six 209 Class (type 1500) submarines (SSK) were ordered from West Germany. Two were completed under licence in Bombay, then the remainder were cancelled in favour of six larger 2000 types. However, these too were later cancelled and construction reverted to the type 1500 of which a final total of four were constructed. Also in 1986 the Soviet Union delivered the first of eight *Kilo* Class attack submarines (SSK) with an option for a further two.

On 3 February, 1988, India joined the 'nuclear club' by leasing from the Soviet Union a *Charlie* I Class SSGN. She was intended to be the lead-boat of a class of from four to six units but she was returned to the Soviet Union in January, 1991, and the whole scheme was abandoned.

There are presently eight *Kilo* Class (SSK), four 209 Type 1500 *Shishumar* Class (SSK) and six *Foxtrot* (SS) in the Indian Navy. In addition there are up to twelve Italian-built two-man SDVs for commando operations.

SUBMARINE INSIGNIA

The Indian submarine insignia was authorized on 8 December, 1967. In appearance it closely resembles that of the United States Navy. The design consists of the state arms, the Pillar of Asoka, with an inward-facing dolphin on either side, all resting on a surf-like base. The badge is made in gold plated metal, measures 71mm x 24mm and has a lug and pin fastening on the reverse. A plastic version is also reported to exist. This is probably reserved for wear on working rig only.

The same device is worn by all ranks and is worn above the pocket on the left-hand breast. There is no official miniature size insignia. Unofficial badges exist in silver metal and in gold bullion embroidery, the latter bearing an anchor, sometimes enclosed in a wreath, below the national emblem and lacking the surf-like base.

Indian submarine qualification insignia, 8 December, 1967.

Indian submarine qualification insignia in light gilt casting and in heavy dull brass casting.

INDONESIA

SUBMARINE SERVICE

Poland supplied Indonesia with its first submarines with the sale, in 1959, of three ex-Soviet *Whiskey* Class (SS). A further four arrived from the USSR in 1962 and eventually fourteen units were acquired. By 1970 only six were operational; of the remainder, six were in reserve and two were being cannibalized for spares. All but three had been disposed of by 1975 and the last one went out of service in the early eighties.

In 1981 two 209 Class (Type 1300) (SSK) were delivered from West Germany. Named the *Cakra* and the *Nanggala,* they are the initial units of a submarine force to eventually number four. It is envisaged that the other two will be similar to the 209s but of larger dimensions. In 1996 the submarine force still comprised only these two boats.

SUBMARINE INSIGNIA

According to official sources two designs of submarine qualification badges have been authorized. The first type appeared in 1959 when the Submarine Force was first formed. It consisted of a joined two piece, gold-coloured, stamped metal badge. This depicted a diving shark surrounded by a circular wreath; overlaid on this was a *Whiskey* Class submarine, on waves, facing the wearer's left. Badges were shipyard-made and varied considerably in detail.

In 1975 the design was changed to the port bow view of a submarine flanked either side by sharks all resting on a representation of waves. It was crudely made of bronze metal and variations in detail frequently occurred. Dimensions could also vary; the following sizes have been noted: 85mm x 24mm, 79mm x 21mm and 78mm x 18mm, plus miniatures measuring 45mm x 13mm and 43mm x 11mm. Fixings could be brooch pins or clutch fasteners. This insignia was also produced in gold embroidered thread on black cloth. For various types of other uniforms other types of cloth badges were also worn. These could be embroidered yellow on black or embroidered yellow edged in brown all on a dark olive rectangle with an inner yellow border. This latter insignia measured 105mm x 37mm overall. No doubt other colour combinations existed. This basic design remains in use today. Again there is considerable variations in details of insignia.

A third type of device can also be found. This may have been an earlier prototype or an unofficial version of the present badge. It is made of bronze metal and depicts a *Whiskey* Class submarine facing the wearer's left with diving sharks either side of the central hull section. It measures 82mm x 35mm.

The same design of qualification badge is awarded to all grades of personnel after successfully completing the one-year Submarine Course. It is worn above the left breast pocket.

Indonesian submarine qualification insignia, original type 1959.

Early Indonesian submarine insignia, dates unknown, possibly a prototype. Design consists of a Whiskey Class submarine and two diving sharks (or dolphins?).

Indonesian submarine qualification insignia 1975.

Indonesian submarine qualification insignia 1975, full size and miniature, showing variations in shark's fins and wave formation.

Cloth versions of Indonesian submarine qualification insignia.

IRAN

SUBMARINE SERVICE

In 1976 the Shah's Government ordered nine submarines, three from the United States of America and six from West Germany. The American submarines, which had formerly served in the US Navy, were of the *Tang* Class (SS). Originating from 1951, they were to be named *Kousseh* (SS101), *Nahang* (SS102) and *Dolfin* (SS103). The submarines from West Germany were to be of the new construction 209 Class (Type 1400).

Imperial Iranian Submarine *Kousseh*, with personnel trained in the

IRAN

US Navy, was commissioned on 19 December, 1978. Shortly afterwards the Shah was overthrown and the boat, still in US waters, was returned to the United States. The other two were then redirected to Turkey. The West Germany order was suspended and eventually cancelled.

In 1987 the new Islamic Republic constructed a miniature submarine based on a combined Germany/Japanese design. This was followed a year later by one of North Korean design. Reports in 1990 and 1991 suggested that two more submarines had been launched. Since then various reports indicate that more midget submarines have been obtained from the former Yugoslavia and it is estimated that these, plus locally made midgets, now number nine.

A Russian *Kilo* Class (SSK) arrived at Bandar Abbas on 13 November, 1992, and was commissioned as *Tareq* (Morning Star) ten days later. A second *Kilo* joined the fleet in 1993. A third is expected to join shortly, with the possibility of a fourth joining at a later date.

SUBMARINE INSIGNIA

The American shipyard that refitted IIS *Kousseh* in 1978 produced insignia closely resembling the unofficial USN SSN badge but incorporating the Shah's crown. The design was of a bow-on view of a modern 'tear drop' submarine with the Imperial Crown above, the central device flanked by dolphins supported on waves. These badges were manufactured in gold plate for officers and in silver plate for ratings. They were fixed by clutch fasteners and measured 75mm x 25mm. Miniatures in both colours were also made. The shipyard presented the badges to the ship's company of IIS *Kousseh* and they were worn, for a short period, on the left upper breast. The commissioning book for the *Kousseh* also showed the same badge on its front cover. When the Monarchy ceased all the badges and commissioning books were ordered to be destroyed. Whether or not this took place is debatable as a fair number of these badges are still available to collectors. It is quite likely that more were manufactured for this purpose. It is clear that they were never an official Iranian issue.

Late in 1992, following the purchase of three *Kilo* Class submarines from Russia, Iranian submariners began to wear insignia in gold and silver. The design was that of a *Kilo* Class submarine facing its wearer's left. Dominating the central part of the badge are the State Arms, which take the form of a religious symbol within a cogged wheel, at the bottom of which are the flukes on an anchor. The basic colour follows that of the rest of the badge, being gold-coloured for officers and silver-coloured for ratings. The religious symbol is normally enamelled in red, though some have been noted in blue on a white central disc. This motif extends over both the sail and hull. Some are manufactured in Russia and these are normally solid brass or white metal, though some white metal examples are in pressed metal. Some of the Russian-made officer's badges have the red religious symbol outlined in blue enamel. The Russian-made badges have screw fixings. Locally made badges are not nearly so well made, they are produced in stamped or pressed metal and have a small, flimsy, brooch fastener. The insignia measures 64mm x 23mm and is believed to be worn on the right breast.

Imperial Iranian submarine qualification insignia, gold for officers and silver for ratings. Though worn, these were quite unofficial having been produced by the American shipyard that had prepared submarines prior to transferring them to the Iranian flag (1978).

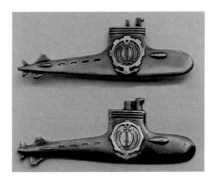

Iranian Islamic Republic submarine qualification insignia about 1990. In brass for officers and in white metal for ratings.

ISRAEL

SUBMARINE SERVICE
The Israeli submarine service began in 1958 with the purchase of two ex-Royal Navy S Class submarines. They were named *Rahav* (ex-HMS

Sanguine) and *Anin* (ex-HMS *Springer*); both remained in service until the early seventies. A further three submarines were purchased from Great Britain between 1967 and 1968. These were of the T Class and were given the names *Leviathan* (ex-HMS *Turpin*), *Dolphin* (ex-HMS *Truncheon*) and *Dakar* (ex-HMS *Totem*). The *Dakar* was subsequently lost in the Mediterranean on 25 January, 1968.

Three IKL Vickers Type 206 (later redesignated Type 540) patrol submarines (SSK) were ordered in 1972 to replace the S and T classes. The *Gal*, *Tanin*, and *Rahav*, displacing 420 tons and armed with eight 21in torpedo tubes plus Sub-Harpoon, were all commissioned in 1977.

Two, possibly three, 1,550 ton submarines designated *Dolphin* Class (SSK) (similar to the German 212 Class but improved) have been ordered from Germany. The projected completion date is 1999.

Submarine Insignia

On the formation of the Israeli submarine arm (in 1958) an insignia was authorized for qualified submarine crews. The original design was of an S Class submarine facing the wearer's right, over which was a centralized motif of a dagger, anchor and laurel wreath spray. It was stamped in light silver-coloured metal, measured 80mm x 36mm, and it had a single screw fixing. A smaller size (not miniature) was also produced measuring 66mm x 29mm and had two clutch fasteners. Shortly afterwards a senior grade insignia was produced. This was the same as the basic badge but was surmounted by the Star of David. The insignia was worn on the left breast above medal ribbons.

In the mid to late 1970s the insignia was altered so that the submarine resembled the more streamlined 540 Class. The central motif remained the same. The insignia came in two grades and two sizes, though the miniature version was unofficial. The basic design was the same as the previous badge apart from the hull form. It measured 75mm x 37mm. The back fixing could be either a single screw and circular nut or two clutch fasteners. The miniature, measuring 40mm x 17mm, had a brooch fixing. There were three versions of it: with the lower part of the anchor voided, non-voided, and made of heavier, more solid metal, probably privately purchases. At the same time a senior insignia was also authorised (termed The Veteran's Badge); it was the same as the standard badges but a laurel wreath arched over the sail and was joined at the top by the Star of David. It measures 75mm x 36mm and again is produced voided and non-voided. In 1992 the basic submarine badge was also made to include the Star of David. Some badges are mounted on a coloured plastic profiled background, mid-blue for war service and red for combat service (other than war service).

Israeli submarine qualification insignia, all ranks 1958.

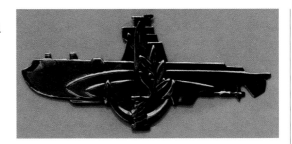

Israeli submarine qualification insignia, all ranks 1958 (80mm x 65mm).

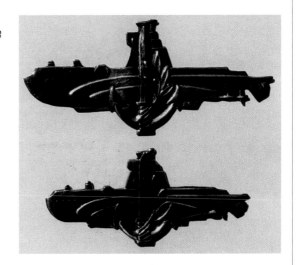

Israeli submarine qualification insignia, second pattern, late 1970s. Full size and miniature, non-voided.

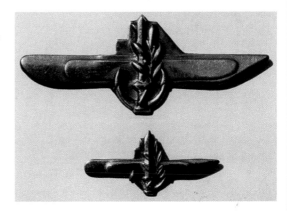

Israeli submarine qualification insignia for veteran, second pattern, voided, late 1970s.

Israeli submarine qualification insignia, with blue plastic profiled backing for combat in war.

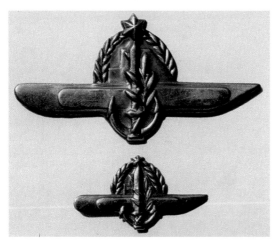

Israeli submarine qualification insignia for veteran, full size and miniature non-voided. Late seventies.

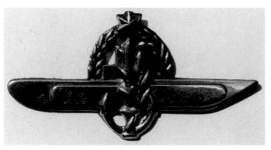

Israeli submarine qualification insignia, second pattern, late 1970s, voided, for veterans.

*Israeli submarine qualifica-
tion insignia with Star of
David 1992.*

ITALY

ROYAL ITALIAN NAVY SUBMARINE SERVICE

The first Italian submarine was the Pullino-designed *Delfino* which entered service in 1895. She displaced 95 tons and was armed with a single torpedo.

Between 1903 and 1905 five Laurenti-designed boats designated the *Glauco* Class were added to the fleet. They displaced 150 tons and were armed with two torpedo tubes. These were followed by five classes of submarines displacing between 180 and 250 tons. Totalling fourteen units, all were armed with two torpedo tubes.

When Italy entered World War I she had twenty submarines in service and eight building. War construction added eight new classes. At the conclusion of hostilities the submarine arm consisted of eleven ocean-going submarines, thirty-five coastal submarines (including seven Canadian-built H Class) and three mine-laying submarines, one of which was ex-Austro-Hungarian. In addition there were thirty-one older boats that were paid off within the year. Ten ex-German U-Boats were ceded to Italy after the Armistice.

Between the wars Italy concentrated on the production of large cruising submarines for the protection of its overseas empire. These ocean-going boats were also seen as a cheap alternative to battleships. Among them was the *Ettore Fieramosca*. Built in 1929, she was, at the time, the world's largest submarine. Designed to carry a sea plane, she was never delivered. When the Empire collapsed these large submarines were found to be unsuitable for Mediterranean deployment. A crash programme was, therefore, commenced to produce smaller types.

Some twelve classes were laid down between the wars. Most of these classes had only two to four units. Nevertheless, it gave Italy the largest submarine fleet of the day.

Production fell off during World War II and only three classes totalling about nineteen submarines were completed. Italy failed to appreciate the strategic value of the submarine on mercantile warfare. Though technically the Italian submarines were probably the world's best, they were not effectively used.

A field in which the Italians did excel was in the use of midget submarines and human torpedoes. Wartime production of these included twenty-six midget submarines (first developed in 1935-6) and over eighty SLCs (*silvro a lento corsa*, or slow course) torpedoes. These were two-man torpedoes or chariots.

After the defeat of Italy thirteen of her submarines came under Allied operational control. At the war's end the Italian Navy mustered sixty-eight submarines including five midgets. Shortly thereafter the submarine branch ceased to exist.

The branch was reactivated in 1954 with the transfer of two ex-USN *Gato* Class submarines. Between 1952 and 1955 five ex-wartime submarines were either completed or reconditioned and entered service. The first Italian-built post-war submarines were the four units of the *Toti* Class (originally SS, later upgraded to SSK) constructed between 1968 and 1969. They were hunter-killer boats of 460 tons armed with four 21in torpedo tubes. Between 1979 and 1982 four more Italian-built submarines entered service. These were of the highly successful *Sauro* Class (Type 1081) (SSK) of 1,456 tons armed with six 21in torpedo tubes. A further four improved *Sauro*s capable of firing the Harpoon missile were commissioned between 1988 and 1994. A possible further order for two larger Type 212 *Sauro* Class units is under consideration.

The present submarine force (1996) consists of four improved *Sauro* Class (SSK), four *Sauro* Class (Type 1081) (SSK) and two *Toti One* (Type 1075)(SSK). The future is uncertain as the projected number of units is to be cut from ten to eight.

ROYAL ITALIAN NAVY SUBMARINE INSIGNIA

Many and varied have been the insignia relating to the Italian Submarine Service. The first device was worn between 1915 and 1918 by junior ratings only. It was regarded as a trade badge and was worn on the left sleeve above rank and branch badges. The insignia was manufactured in silvered metal and depicted a leaping dolphin, facing the wearer's left, encircled by a broad band with a voided background. The top of the band bore the inscription '*Sommergibili*'. The letters were normally painted in dark blue and more rarely in pale blue or black. The entire device was surmounted by the Royal Crown. It measured 45mm (diameter) x 65mm (diameter plus crown) though these dimensions could vary slightly. It was held in position by two fastenings on the back locked by a pin or brooch.

On 16 January, 1918, the device was changed so that the dolphin faced in the other direction (towards the wearer's right) and the Royal Crown was removed.

Officers and chief petty officers were authorized to wear a Submarine Duty Badge on 25 September, 1924. This consisted of a small gilt device worn on the left breast 10mm above, or in place of, medal ribbons. It was similar in design to the original junior rating's trade badge of 1915 but measured 15mm (diameter) x 20mm (diameter plus crown), though this too could vary slightly, some measuring as much as 17mm in diameter. This device could only be worn during the period of assignment to submarines.

On 11 November, 1941, a larger insignia was instituted for officers and chief petty officers. Designated the Submarine Honour Badge, it was similar in design to the Duty Badge, but 25mm (diameter) x 37mm (diameter plus crown) and the lower part of the circular band was in the form of a semi-laurel wreath. It was originally awarded for three war patrols, but later, if this qualification was lacking, it could be awarded for five years' service in submarines. The Honour Badge was made retroactive to include World War I and the Spanish Civil War and it could be worn for life.

During World War II junior ratings wore a special cloth insignia on the left breast of the grey-green working rig. It consisted of a black disc approximately 65mm in diameter on which was a leaping dolphin in yellow, facing the wearer's left.

Italian submariners who were based at Bordeaux and operated in the Atlantic from 1941 to 1943 were granted a special insignia. For officers, warrant officers and senior petty officers the gilt Duty and Honour badges had a red enamelled capital letter 'A' superimposed on the dolphin and the junior rating's silver badge had a 12mm high blue enamelled capital letter 'A' similarly positioned. The letter 'A' also appeared centrally or below or above the dolphin and the crown could vary in detail.

On 11 December, 1943, a series of nine special war service badges were authorized for various elements of the Royal Italian Navy. For the submarine service it was designated the *Distintivo D'Honore Per Lunga Navigazione in Guerra*. The design consisted of a flattened diamond shape with curved sides surmounted by a royal crown. In the centre was a shark facing the wearer's left below which was a torpedo, both superimposed on an anchor. The background was voided. It was awarded in

ITALY

bronze for 18 months embarkation in a submarine or 1,000 hours at sea with at least one engagement with the enemy, in silver for 30 months or 3,000 hours with three engagements and in gold for 48 months or 5,000 hours with six engagements. The insignia was allowed to be worn after the war. Its dimensions were 49mm x 47mm. Its original shape was oval.

In common with surface ships, many wartime submarines had individual badges. These were later manufactured in metal as lapel badges to be worn on civilian clothes. These usually took the form of a voided circular band bearing the submarine's name and, across the centre of and extending beyond the edges, a submarine. The whole was surmounted by a royal crown.

Cap ribbons worn by junior ratings in peacetime indicated the name of the submarine prefixed by SMG. In wartime only the word 'SOMMER-GIBILI' was worn. In common with other Italian cap tallies a star appeared at each end of the lettering. The same system remained after the republic was declared in 1946.

A special device was worn by Italian personnel serving in submarines on loan to Nationalist Spain during the Spanish Civil War. It took the form of an *Archimede* Class submarine, facing the wearer's right, bearing a Royal Crown in the centre (mid-way between the hull and conning tower). Behind the submarine was the insignia of the Spanish (Foreign) Legion. The insignia was worn on the left breast and was in gilt metal for officers, warrant officers and senior petty officers and in silver metal for junior ratings. Two *Archimede* Class submarines, the *Archimede* and *Galilei* and two *Perla* Class submarines the *Onice* and *Iride*, were transferred to Spain in 1936 and 1937 and re-named *General Sanjuro*, *General Mola*, *Avillar Tablada* and *Gonzalaz Lopez*. All were returned to Italy after the Nationalist victory.

(left) Italian officer's, warrant officer's and senior rating's Submarine Duty Badge authorized 1924. 15mm x 20mm.

(right) Italian officer's, warrant officer's and senior rating's Submarine Honour Badge authorized 1941. 25mm x 37mm.

(left) Italian junior rating's trade badge 1915-20.

Italian junior rating's sleeve badge authorized in 1920 and still worn.

(right) Italian junior rating's wartime submarine patch worn on the left breast of the grey-green working rig.

Italian Royal Navy Submarine Service Special War Service Badge in Silver. Authorized 1943.

(right) Italian Submarine Duty Badge, Atlantic, worn by officers, warrant officers and senior ratings 1941-3. Submarine Honour badge similar. Personnel based at Bordeaux. 15mm x 20mm

Submarine insignia worn by officers, warrant officers and senior petty officers serving in submarines on loan to Nationalist Spain during the Spanish Civil War. Junior ratings' insignia was the same but in silver.

Italian junior rating's submarine qualification badge, Atlantic, worn by personnel based at Bordeaux 1941-3.

ITALIAN SOCIALIST REPUBLIC SUBMARINE SERVICE
SEPTEMBER 1943 TO MAY 1945 (*REPUBBLICA SOCIALE ITALIANA* — RSI)

It is difficult to ascertain the exact number of submarines that served in the RSI Navy — there cannot have been many. A Fascist Honour Badge was authorized for the Battle of the Atlantic; whether this was to be worn retroactively or worn by personnel actively engaged, is open to speculation. At the time of the Italian Armistice (9 September, 1943) three Italian submarines were seized by the Germans at their Bordeaux base. It is possible that one or more of these continued to serve under Fascist colours. At the same time thirteen others were captured by the Germans in Italian ports and two were captured by the Japanese. These figures do not include submarines captured while still under construction. Though possible, it is unlikely that any of these served with the RSI. What is known is that ten CB Class four-man midget submarines, captured by the Germans, were transferred to the RSI Navy. They mainly operated in the Adriatic. One was used for spares, seven more were sunk or otherwise destroyed and two were captured by the Allies.

ITALIAN SOCIALIST REPUBLIC SUBMARINE INSIGNIA

RSI Navy personnel continued to wear the former insignia of the Royal Navy but with the royal crown removed. The ratings' silver badge also appeared in bronze.

On 27 May, 1944, the Navy of the RSI authorized the wearing of the nine special war service badges previously authorized by the Royal Italian Navy. The design was the same but without the royal crown. The qualifications for the awards were the same as before.

An Honour Badge was introduced on 27 May, 1944, for submarine crews who took part in the Battle of the Atlantic. It bore a bow view of a submarine, above which was a horizontal *fasces* in the centre of which was a disc bearing a Swastika. A wide oval border carried the inscription '*Atlantico Fedelta 8 Settembre 1943*'. The badge was made of silver metal with the background of a blue sky.

A special badge was also produced for subaqua assault swimmers that was not specifically a submarine badge, but allied to it. It depicted an arm thrust up from the sea grasping a harpoon. It was surrounded by combined wreath and scroll bearing the inscription '*Mezzi de Assalto*'. At the top there was an anchor in the centre of which was a disc bearing the letter 'X^a' (10th Flotilla). It was made in greyish metal.

Towards the end of the war an Atlantic Division Combat sleeve badge was created. It took the form of a frosted silver metal shield 48mm x 79mm depicting a dolphin swimming around a short Roman sword below which was inscribed '*Divisione Atlantica*'. The device had five small holes to enable it to be sewn to the uniform. It was intended for Italian naval personnel (of the RSI) serving at the Atlantic bases of Germany and France from which Italian submarines operated and who stayed behind to combat the advancing Allied troops.

Numerous other special badges were created to commemorate various combat units. Most took the form of a submarine on waves surrounded by a combined wreath and scroll. Many included the letter 'X^a' in the design. (See the illustration of the Barbarigo Battalion.)

The elite SCIRE Submarine Battalion from 1943 to 1945 wore a gold device resembling the silver rating's badge but with the letter 'X^a' (10th) centrally located just above the dorsal fin of the dolphin. The wording on the outer band was '*Btg Sommergibili SCIRE*'.

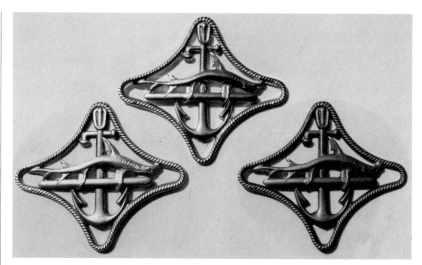

Italian Submarine Service Special War Badge (Distintivo D'Honore Per Lunga Navigazione In Guerra) gold, silver and bronze, authorized in 1944. (Frogman's badge is similar but shark replaced by a frogman astride a 'human torpedo'). Italian Socialist Republic.

Italian Socialist Republic Distinction of Honour for the Barbarigo Battalion, Nettuna Front. Scroll at the top bears the inscription 'FRONTE DI NETTUNO'.

(right) Italian Socialist Republic sleeve insignia for service in the Atlantic Division.

REPUBLIC OF ITALY SUBMARINE INSIGNIA

Since the Republic was declared in 1946, submarine insignia has remained in much the same design as in the former Royal Navy but without the crown.

Since 1948 the Italian submarine qualification insignia comes in three sizes. Officers and senior ratings wear the design of 1924 and 1941 without the crown and junior ratings the same design as for 1920 (this comes in chrome or frosted silver). Officers and senior ratings wear the Duty Badge measuring 15mm in diameter and the Honour Badge measuring 25mm in diameter. The junior ratings' sleeve badge is 45mm in diameter. Two unofficial badges exist. One, an Honour Badge 55mm in diameter, is said to be worn by some senior officers (but this is not confirmed), and the other a standard-size Honour Badge surmounted by a mural crown* is worn as a beret badge only.

In 1990 the Duty and Honour badges had a naval crown** added, making them look very much like the beret badge but smaller.

An unidentified badge has recently appeared, being of the same design and materials as the rating's badge of 1920 but of the size now worn by officers. This may be a commemorative badge.

---

* Mural Crown — a three-turreted castle.
** Naval Crown — similar to the mural crown but with an anchor superimposed on the central turret and with representations of the prow of a Roman galley below the two other turrets and extending either side of the base.

Italian Republic officer's, warrant officer's and senior rating's Submarine Duty Badge 1948-90, then Naval Crown added. 15mm diameter.

(above, right) Italian Republic officer's, warrant officer's and senior rating's Submarine Honour Badge 1948-90, then Naval Crown added. 25mm diameter.

Italian Republic admiral's large (unofficial) Submarine Honour Badge (55mm diameter).

Italian Republic submarine service insignia for junior ratings, 1948, in chrome and frosted silver. 45mm diameter.

Italian Republic submarine qualification insignia with naval crown, authorized in 1990 for officers, warrant officers and senior ratings, (25mm x 33mm and 17mm x 21mm).

Italian Republic submarine beret badge, with mural crown. 24 x 35mm.

JAPAN

SUBMARINE SERVICE

Early Japanese submarines were based on British, German and French designs. The submarine arm commenced in 1904 with the purchase from Great Britain of five elementary Holland type boats. Numbered 1 to 5, they had a submerged displacement of 120 tons, were 65ft long and were armed with a single 18in torpedo tube. The next vessels were built in Japan two years later and were numbered 6 and 7. These were of 180 tons, 100ft long and armed with three 18in torpedo tubes. Numbers 8 and 9, British built, were added in 1907 and 1908. Displacing 320 tons, they were similar to the British C Class. Of the same type, numbers 10 to 15 were constructed in Japan. France built numbers 16 and 17 just before World War I. All seventeen were serving in the Imperial Japanese Navy at the onset of war.

War construction amounted to less than twelve additions. Like the rest of the Japanese Navy, after mopping up Germany's few possessions in the Pacific and Far East, they spent the remainder of World War I on patrol duties in the Pacific. At the end of hostilities Japan was allocated six ex-German ocean-going and two ex-German mine-laying submarines. They were used for experimental purposes only and were not commissioned into the fleet.

In order to counter American Naval supremacy in the Pacific between the wars Japan commenced a large submarine construction programme. For the most part these new vessels were large ocean-going cruising boats capable of long endurance at sea, a necessity in the vast expanses of the Pacific. They also featured deep-diving capabilities and many were fitted with a catapult and sea-plane and 5.5in guns.

Japan entered the war in 1941 with fifty-six front line submarines and some seventeen older craft used for training and ancillary purposes. Well over sixty-five were building or on order. War construction added sixty-seven large, medium and coastal submarines. Among them were a number of specialist types: supply submarines which could carry cargo, landing craft and amphibious tanks, ocean-going submarines which could carry midget submarines and human torpedoes, command submarines with special telecommunication facilities and tanker submarines for refuelling sea-planes and flying boats. The I 400 Class, when completed in 1944, were, at 5,223 tons, the world's largest underwater vessels. They carried three bombing air-craft and had a range of 30,000 nautical miles at 14 knots. They shipped dummy funnels to disguise themselves when 'steaming' on the surface and had an endurance of ninety days. In addition, two classes of unarmed supply submarines were built by the Army and well over two hundred midget submarines were built by the Navy. These midget craft displaced between 46 and 60 tons, were normally armed with two 18in torpedoes and had a complement of two to five men. The value of the submarine in mercantile warfare was ignored to Japan's cost. The submarine force was, for the most part, used as scouts for the fleet and for attacking enemy fleet formations. Their failure to utilize the submarine as a commerce raider was reflected by the poor results achieved. Just over two hundred Allied vessels were sunk throughout the war. Little heed was paid to anti-submarine warfare and as a result the Japanese submarines suffered grievously at the hands of the USN A/S escorts.

As a last desperate measure hundreds of one-man and two-man suicide craft (human torpedoes) styled *Kaiten* were constructed. They displaced between 8 and 18 tons and carried a 3,428lb warhead. They came too late and achieved little tangible results.

Some one hundred and twenty-five Japanese submarines were lost during the conflict. Fifty-eight, including six ex-German and two ex-Italian boats, were surrendered. All were subsequently broken up by the Allied Powers.

Following Japan's defeat her armed forces were disintegrated and the nation was demilitarized. In 1954 the Japanese Maritime Self Defence Force was formed, a navy in everything but name.

The first submarine of this new force was an ex-USN *Gato* Class (SS) the *Kuroshio* (ex-USS *Mingo*), commissioned into the JMSDF in 1955 and deleted in 1966. All further submarines to enter the service were Japanese designed and built.

The first of these 'all Japanese' submarines was a one-ship prototype Class the *Oyashio* (SS). She was launched in 1959 and displaced 1,100 tons. Her weapon fit was four 19.7in torpedo tubes. She continued in service until 1976. *Oyashio* was followed by the four-ship *Hayashio/Natsushio* Class (SS) of 750 tons displacement and armed with three 21in torpedo tubes. They were launched between 1961 and 1962 and were finally deleted by 1987. The five *Ooshio* Class (SS) of 1,600 tons armed with eight 21in torpedo tubes were launched between 1964 and 1968 and continued in service until 1968. These were followed by the six-ship *Uzushio* Class (SS) of 1,850 tons displacement and armed with six 21in torpedo tubes. They were launched between 1970 and 1975. Three were paid off by 1991. Two later classes are the ten ship *Yuushio* Class (SSK) of 2,200 tons displacement armed with six 21in torpedo tubes launched between 1979 and 1988 and the seven *Harushio* Class (SSK) launched between 1989 and 1995. These 2,450 ton displacement submarines are armed with six 21in torpedo tubes which are also capable of launching Sub Harpoon SSM.

The first unit of an improved *Harushio* Class of 2,500 tons displacement was laid down in 1993 and will enter service in 1998. It is anticipated that others will follow on in twelve month intervals.

The submarine force at the time of writing (1996) comprises one improved *Harushio* Class (SSK), six *Harushio* Class (SSK), ten *Yuushio* Class (SSK) and two *Uzuhio* Class (S) used for training.

SUBMARINE INSIGNIA

From 1932 petty officers and junior ratings who had completed the course in the Submarine Training School were entitled to wear a special insignia. This consisted of a rudimentary representation of a submarine in silver facing its wearer's right. It was superimposed on a 38mm diameter nut-brown (some were orange-brown) cherry blossom by means of a bolt the head of which was peined over the centre of the reverse of the blossom (on reproductions this head was either stuck on, or missing altogether). The cherry blossom flower was fairly thick and the blossom segments in section were convex. The insignia was fixed to the uniform by means of a horizontal flat hinged pin secured by a single hook and was worn on the right side of the uniform jacket approximately mid-way between collar and skirt. Unofficial sources indicate the existence of a similar device for officers but with a gold submarine. This is thought to be unlikely. On security grounds the insignia ceased to be worn in 1940 and was abolished altogether in 1942. Few originals survived as they were required to be returned to stores in 1942 and most were melted down for other purposes.

There were also various other symbols associated with the submarine. One of these was an arm or head band made in white linen, printed with orange and black stripes top and bottom. In the centre was a ship's screw within a circle and with Japanese characters for *Gaku-To* on either side. This stood for 'Youth who learn at university'. It was worn by ex-students who volunteered to serve in small submarines, including human torpedoes. It was said to contain 'the soul of the owner'.

In June, 1961, after the formation of the Japanese Maritime Self Defence Force, a submarine qualification badge was authorized. This insignia is the same design for both officers and ratings, though in the case of officers it is gold and in the case of ratings it is silver. The insignia, manufactured in metal of the appropriate colour, comprises a central motif of a cherry blossom on the shank of an anchor; inward-facing dolphins are on each side. Anchor, cherry blossoms and dolphins rest on symbolic waves. The device closely resembles the submarine badge of the US Navy. It is produced in two sizes, 70mm x 22mm and 60mm x 21mm. Both brooch and clutch fastening can be used for securing the insignia which is worn by all ranks on the left upper breast.

Japanese Imperial Navy insignia for completion of training at The Naval Submarine School, 1932-45.

Japanese Imperial Navy unofficial device worn by suicide crews in miniature submarines in 1945.

JMSDF submarine qualifica-tion insignia, in gold, for officers.
Top: 70mm in gilded gold. Bottom: 61mm in standard gold. Authorized June, 1961.

JMSDF submarine qualification insignia in silver for
ratings.
Top: 70mm in standard
silver.
Bottom: 61mm in frosted
silver.
Authorized June, 1961.

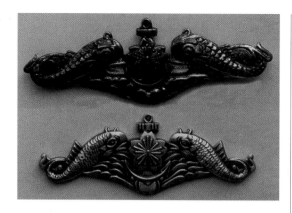

DEMOCRATIC PEOPLE'S REPUBLIC OF KOREA (NORTH KOREA)

SUBMARINE SERVICE

The submarine service was formed in late 1959 with the acquisition from the Soviet Union of two *Whiskey* Class submarines (SS). This number was increased to four by the end of the decade. By 1991 all four had been reduced to a training role.

In 1973 two Chinese-built *Romeo* Class submarines (SS) were added to the underwater fleet followed by a further two in 1974 and three more in 1975. These were followed by similar boats built in North Korea of which one was lost off the East coast of Korea in 1985. By 1993 only two of the original Chinese-built boats remained in service but the North Korean-built boats numbered twenty-four.

In addition to conventional submarines, some ten coastal submarines have been built since 1988. Reported to be of Yugoslav design, some have been built and are termed the *Sang-o* Class. They displace 76 tons surfaced and can carry limpet mines and or combat swimmers. Over fifty-five submarines (SDV) have also been locally constructed since 1974. Their function is to land small clandestine commando units behind enemy lines.

Between 1993 and 1994 thirty old Russian submarines were delivered to North Korea for 'scrapping'. These consisted of F, GII, R and W Classes (SS).

KOREA

The present submarine force consists of between twenty-two and twenty-four *Romeo* Class (SS), ten small coastal submarines (SSC) and fifty midget submarines (SDV).

Submarine Insignia

No information is available on submarine insignia. It is unlikely that any exist.

Republic of Korea (South Korea)

Submarine Service

Three KSS-1 *Tolgorae* Class and eight *Cosmos* Class (Italian designed) midget submarines have been constructed with the first entering service in 1983. The former are armed with two 406mm torpedo tubes and the latter with two 533mm torpedo tubes. Both displace 150 tons surfaced, but the *Cosmos* are primarily SDVs.

In 1987 three 209 (Type 1200) submarines (SSK) were ordered from West Germany. To be known as *Chang Bogo* Class, the first was constructed in Germany and entered service in 1993. The other two were constructed in the ROK and were commissioned in 1994 and 1995. 1989 and 1993 saw the ordering of two further batches of three, all to be built in the ROK. All should be in service by 1999.

Submarine Insignia

Submarine qualification badges were authorized on 17 September, 1992, gold for officers and silver for ratings. The design is similar to the USN insignia and shows a bow-on view of a submarine either side of which are inward-facing dolphins supported either side of the submarine on four upward and outward sloping stylized waves. The prow of the submarine bares the ROK National symbol, the *Yin Yang* disc, below which appears the bottom portion of an anchor.

These badges are also embroidered in gold and silver on dark cloth and dimensions are 62mm x 23mm and a miniature version also exists. The device is worn on the left upper breast, by means of two clutch fasteners. Qualifications required are a seven-month specialist course, employment in submarines or an appointment as a Submarine Squadron Staff Officer.

*Republic of Korea subma-
rine qualification insignia,
gold for officers and silver
for ratings. Authorized 17
September, 1992.*

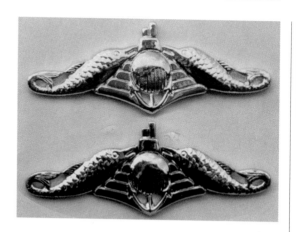

LATVIA

SUBMARINE SERVICE
In the early 1920s two coastal submarines were ordered from France. Named *Ronis* and *Spidola* they entered service in 1926. Armed with six 17.7in torpedo tubes and eight guns they displaced 390 tons and were 180.5ft long.

Difficulties in maintenance and lack of qualified personnel led to the vessels being laid up. When war came both were unserviceable. They were seized by Soviet Forces in June, 1940.

SUBMARINE INSIGNIA
It is unlikely that any specialist insignia ever existed. However, cap ribbons bore the submarine's name or indicated that the wearer was serving in the Submarine Division.

LIBYA

SUBMARINE SERVICE

The submarine service was formed in 1976 with the acquisition of the first of six Soviet *Foxtrot* Class (SS) the last of which entered service in 1983. One was subsequently deleted in 1992 and another was lost in 1993.

Two Yugoslav R2 *Mala* Class miniature free-flood submarines, similar to the British wartime torpedo-shaped Chariots, were delivered in 1977. These were followed by two more in 1981 and a further two in 1982, with others possibly to follow.

SUBMARINE INSIGNIA

Little information is known about any specialist submarine insignia. A cloth badge is said to have been authorized about 1990. This depicts a simple submarine design, facing the wearer's right embroidered in gold wire on a black contoured backing. It measures 71mm x 22mm and is fixed to the uniform with either a pin-back or a screw-on device. A metal version was produced in about 1994 which more closely resembles a *Foxtrot* Class submarine.

Libyan submarine qualification insignia gold wire embroidery on black cloth.

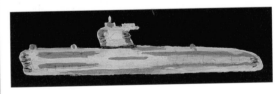

Libyan submarine qualification insignia in brass, in the style of a Foxtrot Class submarine.

MALAYSIA

SUBMARINE SERVICE

In late 1988 the Malaysian Government ordered an ex-Royal Navy *Oberon* Class submarine from Great Britain, but it was never delivered.

In the spring of 1991 the Royal Malaysian Navy ordered four submarines from Sweden, two reconditioned ex-Swedish Navy *Draken* Class dating from the 1960s, one to be used for sea training and the other for alongside training, and two of the latest A19 Type boats. In 1992 the programme was postponed. A 1994 report suggested that a possible six ex-UK *Oberon* Class submarines might be purchased and that some personnel had already been trained. This purchase is now unlikely to materialize, though there is a strong move to acquire submarines in the near future. Malaysian Naval personnel are presently (1996) receiving submarine training in Australia, India and Pakistan.

SUBMARINE INSIGNIA

Malaysian naval officers have been trained in Germany, the United Kingdom, Sweden, Australia, Pakistan and India. It is possible that some may have qualified for submarine insignia for those countries. To date no information is available regarding the existence of similar Malaysian insignia. In 1994 it was rumoured that 'trained personnel' were wearing Australian dolphins.

NETHERLANDS

SUBMARINE SERVICE

The world's first submarine was built by a Dutchman, Cornelius Drebbel, in 1620. The first submarine to enter Dutch naval service was simply designed Boat No1. It displaced 120 tons and was armed with one torpedo tube. It entered service in 1905. Between 1910 and 1912 a further nine boats in three classes were added to the Navy. They had a surface displacement of between 131 and 380 tons and were armed with two torpedo tubes.

As the need for larger long-range submarines arose in order to protect the Netherlands Overseas colonies, submarines were identified by either K (*Kolonien*) for colonial service or O (*Onderzeeboot*) for home service before their numerals. The K-boats were of at least 500 tons displacement as opposed to the smaller O-boats which were deployed in or near the North Sea. This system remained until 1937 when submarine areas of operation become interchangeable and the K and O prefixes were dropped.

Eleven classes consisting of both categories were added to the Navy between 1913 and 1920. These included an ex-British H Class interned in 1916 and subsequently purchased and an ex-German minelaying type purchased in 1917.

By 1931 there were twenty-two submarines in service and nine building. Of those building the 021 class, commenced in 1937 and ready for service just before the war, were the world's first submarines to incorporate a telescopic breathing tube so that the submarine could cruise at periscope depth under diesel power. The Germans later developed this, from examples found in Rotterdam in 1943, into what became famous as the schnorkel.

When war commenced there were thirty submarines in Dutch service. Six were captured in Dutch ports and four were to be sunk or scuttled due to enemy action. After Japan's entry into the war a further six were sunk or scuttled due to action with Japanese Forces. In all, fourteen Dutch submarines escaped to the Allies either to survive the war or to be scrapped in Allied yards as of no further use. Four British submarines (HMS/Ms *Sturgeon*, *Talent*, *Tarn* and P47) were transferred to the Dutch flag during the war.

The first post-war submarines to join the Netherlands submarine service were two ex-USN *Walrus* Class (ex-USS *Icefish* and ex-US *Hawksbill* later restyled *Balao* Class) (SS). They were transferred on loan for a five-year period commencing in 1953. These were followed by four Dutch-built submarines of the *Potvis* Class (SS), later subdivided into two classes of two submarines each (known as the *Potvis/Zeehond* Class). They had a surface displacement of 1,200 tons and were armed with eight 21in torpedo tubes. All entered service between 1961 and 1966.

The *Zwaardvis* Class (SSK) of two submarines was completed in 1972. Of 2,350 tons surface displacement, they are armed with six 21in torpedo tubes.

The latest class, an improved *Zwaardvis* design, is the *Walrus* Class (SSK). They have a surface displacement of 2,450 tons and are armed with four 21in torpedo tubes and Harpoon missiles. By early 1994 all four were in commission and constitute the present submarine force.

Both *Zwaardvis* Class were put up for sale in 1993 and will be available by 1996. The remaining *Potvis/Zeehond* Class have been relegated to other duties or disposed of.

SUBMARINE INSIGNIA

The Dutch submarine badge was authorized on 24 February, 1965, though it was not worn until the early 1970s. The wearing of the insignia is not compulsory.

The design comprises two outward-facing dolphins, with tails crossed, supporting the bow view of a modern Royal Netherlands Navy submarine. It is made in gilt metal measuring 62mm x 22mm and is fixed either by a hinged pin or by clutch fastenings. An unofficial gold bullion variation also exists. There is also an unofficial miniature in metal. It measures 25mm long and it has a brooch fastening.

The same device is worn by all ranks serving in submarines or in the submarine service. It is worn on the left breast below medal ribbons if worn.

NETHERLANDS

Netherlands submarine qualification insignia for all ranks, 24 February, 1965.

Netherlands submarine qualification insignia embroidered on uniform in gold wire.

NORWAY

SUBMARINE SERVICE

Norway formed its submarine service in 1908 with the acquisition from Germany of a small submarine of the Krupp Germania Type. This boat entered service in 1909 as the *Kobben* but was shortly redesignated A1.

A further four, slightly larger, boats were ordered from Germany to be designated A2, A3, A4 and A5. The first three were delivered in 1913. However, A5 was appropriated by Germany on the outbreak of war in 1914.

In the mid to late 1920s Norway constructed six submarines of the Holland Type, designated B1 to B6. It was with this class of 413 tons surface displacement with four torpedo tubes that Norway entered the war in 1940, the previous A Class having been decommissioned by 1931.

All the B boats fell into German hands with the exception of B1 which was scuttled in Ofotfjord to escape falling into enemy hands. She was raised after the Second Battle of Narvik and escaped to join the free Norwegian Forces in Britain.

The Royal Navy transferred five U Class submarines to the Norwegian ensign between 1943 and 1944. All survived the war to serve in the post-war Norwegian Navy, the last being broken up in 1965.

Three German VII C Type U-boats were ceded to Norway at the end of the hostilities, the last one being taken out of service in 1964.

In the early 1960s a new class of fifteen submarines was ordered from West Germany. In order to train crews for these new boats, West Germany loaned a similar type, the U3, to Norway for a period of two years. She was temporarily re-named *Kobben* while serving under the Norwegian colours.

These new vessels, designated the 207 (or *Kobben*) Class, are small coastal attack submarines (SSK). They are driven by diesel and electric engines with a surface displacement of 370 to 435 tons and are armed with eight 21in torpedo tubes. One was cancelled and the remainder all entered service by 1967. Two were sold to Denmark in 1986 and a third in 1989. One was scrapped in 1989 following an accident. Six were modernized and lengthened by 1989 but apart from these the remainder will gradually be phased out of service.

A new class designated *Ula* Type P6071 (ex-210) (SSK) was contracted in 1982; also German-built, they have a surface displacement of 1,040 tons and are armed with eight 21in torpedo tubes. The six boats of this class all commissioned between 1989 and 1992. They, with the six modernized *Kobben* (Type 207) SSKs form the present (1996) Norwegian submarine force.

Norwegian submarine qualification insignia for officers with twelve months service in submarines, full size and miniature (1958). A more stylizes embroidered insignia has recently emerged to conform more closely with the metal badges.

Norwegian submarine qualification insignia in metal. Top for officer's shirts and bottom for officers with less than 12 month's service and for ratings, all uniforms (1958).

Norwegian Submarine Service cloth badge for wear on sweaters by all ranks. As the submarine faces the other way, it indicates that the badge is worn on the left sleeve.

SUBMARINE INSIGNIA

It was in 1958 that the Royal Norwegian Navy adopted its present style submarine badge. Before that time no specialist insignia was worn. It consists of a royal crown with submarine below, facing the wearer's right. Either side are two inward-facing sea creatures.

The design of the badge is the same for all ranks. For officers who have completed twelve months' service it is embroidered on the dark blue service uniform in gold bullion wire and is available in gold-plated silver with a pin back for wear on khaki or tropical uniforms. Officers who have not qualified for the gold wire badge and all ratings wear a bronze metal badge with a pin fastening. This is awarded after completing the submarine course and having satisfactorily served on board a submarine for six months. The badge is available in two sizes. The standard uniform item measures 60mm x 20mm and an embroidered miniature measuring 40mm x 15mm is available for mess dress.

The submarine insignia is worn on the right-hand side of the chest level with the arm pit. Officers wear the miniature badge on the lapel of the mess dress. A circular cloth badge 98mm in diameter is worn by all personnel on the sleeve of the sweater.

Ratings, dressed as seamen, in the submarine service wear a distinctive cap ribbon bearing the inscription 'KNM UNDERVANNSBAT' (KNM = Kongelige Norske Marine, ie Royal Norwegian Navy Submarine).

PAKISTAN

SUBMARINE SERVICE

The Pakistan Navy began its submarine arm in 1964 with the loan of a submarine from the United States. This was the *Tench* Class (SS) USS *Diablo* renamed *Ghazi* (Defender of the Faith). In 1970 three French *Daphne* Class submarines (SSK) were commissioned. This number was made up to four in 1975 with the acquisition of the Portuguese submarine *Cachalote*, which replaced the *Ghazi*.

During 1972-3 six SX 404 Class midget submarines (SDV) were purchased from Italy. Displacing 40 tons, their main function was to transport up to twelve commando special forces on clandestine raids. One was lost in an accident in 1976, some were discarded in 1982-3 and all were out of service by 1990. They were replaced by three larger midget submarines (SSC) of 110 tons dived displacement. These were the Italian-made SX 756 Type (MG110 Class), armed with two 21in torpedo tubes and can carry eight combat swimmers and explosives plus two SDVs. Italy has also provided Pakistan with a number of two-man chariots.

Originally intended for South Africa, two French *Agosta* Class submarines (SSK) were purchased in 1978. In 1984/5 they were fitted with US Sub-Harpoon anti-ship missiles. In September, 1994, it was announced that three more of this class have been ordered. The first and probably the second are to be built in France and the last in Pakistan.

In 1996 the submarine force stood at two *Hashmat* (*Agosta* Class) SSK, four *Hangor* (*Daphne* Class) SSK and three MG110 (SX 56 Type) SSC.

SUBMARINE INSIGNIA

The submarine insignia was designed in June, 1964. It was manufactured in metal and measures 66mm x 29mm (though this can vary slightly). It is normally secured to the uniform by a hinged brooch pin and hook. For officers it is gilt metal and for ratings silvered or chromed. Ratings on promotion to officer continue to wear the silver badge until they requalify.

The device consists of a submarine facing the wearer's right; around the centre of the submarine is a wreath closed at the top with a star and crescent. The insignia is worn on the left breast above medal ribbons if any.

A miniature, 54mm x 22mm, exists and cloth versions of the full sized insignia are produced, red on blue and blue on white, details on both being picked out in white.

Combat swimmers (Special Service Group) wear a very similar badge. It is similar to the submariners' badge but has an upright dagger in the centre. The grip starts just below the wreath and the blade just touches the crescent. A cloth variation also exists.

Pakistan submarine qualifica-tion insignia in gilt for officers and chrome for ratings. Authorized June, 1964.

PERU

SUBMARINE SERVICE

During the War of the Pacific with Chile in 1879-83 a submersible craft designed by Fredrico Blume was built at the port of Pita. It made several test dives but had to be scuttled to prevent it from falling into enemy hands.

The first true submarines to be commissioned were the French-built Laubeuf Types *Ferre* and *Palacios*. Purchased in 1911, they displaced 300 tons and were armed with one bow torpedo tube. During the period of World War I they became inactive, due to the unavailability of batteries, and were eventually scrapped in 1919.

At the instigation of the US Naval Missions in 1920, four R Class submarines were built in the United States. They were given the designations of R1 to R4 and served until well into the sixties. They displaced 576 tons and were armed with four 21in torpedo tubes and a 3in gun.

Between 1952 and 1957 four US-built submarines based on the *Mackerel* Class (SS) were purchased to form the *Tiburnon* Class (later renamed the *Abtao* Class); one was deleted in 1990. Two more US-built boats were purchased in 1974. These were of the *Guppy* 1A Class (SS) ex-USS *Sea Poacher* and ex-USS *Atule*. They were deleted in 1992 and 1993.

During 1969 two 209 (Type 1200) submarines (SSK) were ordered from West Germany. These were followed by four more of the same class in 1976-7. All were commissioned between 1975 and 1980.

The present force consists of six 209 Class and two *Abtao* Class.

SUBMARINE INSIGNIA

The submarine speciality badge, authorized 8 June, 1949, is produced in metal 73mm x 23mm and is secured to the uniform by a hinged brooch pin and hook. It is produced in gilt for officers and in silver for ratings. Miniatures of both types also exist.

The design consists of an R Class submarine facing the wearer's left. Centrally located towards the bottom of the hull is an enamel shield bearing the national arms in full colour, either side of which is an inward-facing dolphin. Early badges depicted the dolphins and shield just below the submarine's hull; later styles showed them partially on the submarine's hull. The insignia is worn on the left breast above medal ribbons. Originally ratings wore a similar cloth embroidered badge on the left sleeve just below the shoulder seam.

An updated version with a modern submarine is said to exist.

Peruvian submarine qualification insignia for officers in gilt and for ratings in silver. Authorized 8 June, 1949.

POLAND

SUBMARINE SERVICE

The first submarines to sail under the Polish flag were three 980 ton French-built boats which entered service in 1931. These were given the names *Rys*, *Zbik* and *Wilk*. Intended for Baltic service, they had a relatively small radius of action but a substantial torpedo armament and mine-laying capacity.

Just before World War II Poland took delivery of two Dutch-built submarines. These were given the names *Sep* and *Orzel*. Of 1,110 tons their armament and mine-laying capacity was double that of their predecessors.

At the outbreak of war *Sep*, *Rys* and *Zbik* sailed to Sweden and internment. However, *Orzel* and *Wilk* escaped to serve under Allied command. Thus the entire submarine force escaped falling into the hands of the enemy. *Orzel* was lost in 1940 but *Wilk* survived the war.

Three Allied submarines were transferred to the Free Polish Navy; the British U Class submarines P52 and *Urchin* were renamed *Dzik* and *Sokol* and the American PSSI (ex-British S25) was renamed *Jastrzab*. *Dzik* and *Sokol* survived the war but *Jastrzab* was lost in 1942, having struck a mine.

After the war *Dzik* was transferred to Denmark and *Sokol* was returned to Britain. *Rys*, *Wilk* and *Zbik* continued to serve until 1957 and the last of the wartime boats, *Sep*, went out of service in 1971.

With the restructuring of the post-war Polish Navy, six ex-Soviet MV Class submarines (SSC) were acquired between 1956 and 1957. These

POLAND

were replaced by five ex-Soviet *Whiskey* Class (SS), four of which were transferred to Poland between 1962 and 1965 and the fifth some time later. By 1989 all had been withdrawn from service. They were replaced by two former Soviet *Foxtrot*s (SS) in 1987-8.

In 1986 the Soviet Union transferred a *Kilo* Class submarine (SSK) to Poland. The *Kilo* (SS) and the two *Foxtrot*s (SS) constitute the present (1996) Polish submarine arm.

SUBMARINE INSIGNIA

The Polish submarine insignia was authorized in 1964 by Ministry of National Defence Order number 9.

The device is made of lightweight stamped metal secured by a single clutch fastener or a screwed lug. It consists of a conventional submarine facing the wearer's left. Centralized over the hull and conning tower is the Polish eagle below which appear the arms and flukes of an anchor.

The insignia is worn in three colours, gold for commanding and ex-commanding officers, silver for other officers and bronze for ratings. It comes in one size only measuring 70mm x 23mm and all ranks wear the device on the right breast. There can be some variation in detail and quality and the rating's badge is sometimes produced in dull bronze-like very thin metal.

Like the Soviet Navy the Polish Navy produces a number of ship

Polish submarine qualification insignia, in gold-coloured metal for commanding officers, in silver-coloured metal for other officers and in bronze for ratings, (about 1964).

commemorative badges for wear on the right breast. As an example, the first *Kilo* in service had such a badge. This took the form of a wreath on the base of which was a scroll bearing the inscription '*Pierwsza Zatoga 1986*' (First Crew 1986) surmounted by the Polish eagle on a shield and all in silver. Within the wreath from top to bottom was a white sky, a black *Kilo* Class submarine and a red 'sea' which bore the inscription '*Orp Orzel* III' (Polish Republic Ship *Orzel*). The badge which was enamelled measured 30mm x 42mm and had a screw back.

PORTUGAL

Submarine Service

Portugal's submarine history goes back to 1913 when the 245 ton *Espadarte* of the Italian Laurenti type was commissioned. Three more submarines of Italian construction followed in 1916/17. Known as the *Foca* Class (*Foca*, *Golfinho* and *Hidra*) they displaced 260 tons and were armed with two 18in torpedo tubes, similar to the *Espadarte*.

In the early 1930s Italy supplied a further two submarines designated the *Delfim* Class (*Delfim* and *Espadarte*). Considerably larger than their predecessors they displaced 770 tons and were armed with six 21in torpedo tubes. Both remained in service until well into the mid-1940s.

In 1948 three ex-British S Class (HMS/Ms *Spearhead*, *Saga* and *Spur*) were purchased. They were renamed *Neptuno*, *Nautilo* and *Narval* and served until 1967, 1969 and 1979 respectively. This class was followed by the purchase of four French *Daphne* Class submarines (SSK) between 1967 and 1969. One of these, the *Cachalote*, was, sold to Pakistan in 1975.

The present force consists of the three *Daphne* Class submarines *Albacora*, *Barracude* and *Delfim*.

Submarine Insignia

The first submarine insignia was authorized in 1915. It was originally intended for officers only but it was later extended to all ranks. The badge depicted the Navy's first submarine *Espadarte*. It faced the wearer's right and measured 52mm x 31mm. Worn on the right sleeve 50mm below the elbow, it was embroidered in gold for officers and senior ratings and in red on blue or blue on white for junior ratings.

In 1920 the design was altered to feature a *Delfim* Class submarine. This time it faced the wearer's left and measured 91mm x 22mm. Above the conning tower was placed a detached disc displaying the national arms in full colour. At this stage the badge was repositioned for officers and senior ratings to the right side of the upper chest. Junior ratings continued to wear the insignia on the sleeve.

In 1936 the national arms device was removed from the badges worn by senior and junior ratings.

In the mid-1950s a more modern badge appeared for officers and senior ratings. It was made in gilded stamped brass and took the form of a British 'A' Class submarine facing its wearer's left. The official version bore the National Arms in the centre, whereas the one for senior ratings was plain. It measured 63mm x 22mm and was fixed to the uniform by a long brooch fastener. Its authenticity cannot be verified — but it was worn well into the 1960s.

The present more modern hull form design was adopted in 1960 with the national arms device worn by officers surrounded by a wreath. Senior and junior ratings continued to wear it without the national arms device.

In 1961 the national arms device worn by officers was lowered to cover the central part of the submarine. At the same time polished brass badges became available for officers and senior ratings for wear on white uniforms. Junior ratings continued to wear the cloth sleeve badge, red on blue, and blue on white.

The insignia is worn by all qualified submariners and the present badge measures 65mm x 25mm. The metal version has a hinged brooch pin and hook fastener. There is no miniature badge; officers wear the full size badge on mess dress. Both officers and senior ratings can wear a gold embroidered badge on service uniform at their option. Some badges produced later show a slightly more modernized version of the submarine.

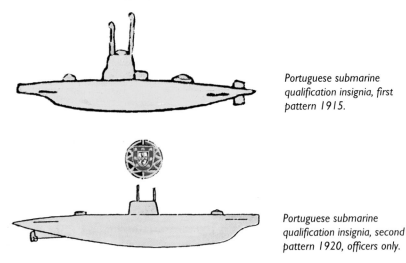

Portuguese submarine qualification insignia, first pattern 1915.

Portuguese submarine qualification insignia, second pattern 1920, officers only.

Portuguese submarine
qualification insignia, 1936
pattern for career petty
officers.

Portuguese submarine
qualification insignia, third
pattern for officers 1960.

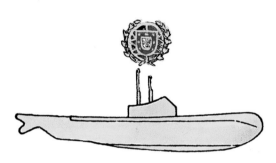

Portuguese submarine
qualification insignia
variation about. 1956 to
1960, for career petty
officers. Officers badge is
the same but with the
National Arms in the centre.

Portuguese submarine
qualification insignia for
officers 1961.

Portuguese submarine
qualification insignia for
career petty officers 1961.

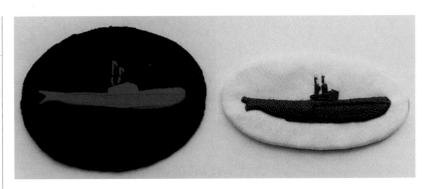

Portuguese submarine qualification insignia for wear on the sleeve by junior ratings.
Embroidered in blue on white cloth for summer or red on dark blue cloth for winter.

ROMANIA

SUBMARINE SERVICE

Romania's first submarine was ordered from Italy in 1927, completed in 1931 and entered service in 1936. Named *Delfinul,* she had a surface displacement of 650 tons and was armed with six 21in torpedo tubes plus one 4in gun.

The next submarine to enter service was the *Marsuinul.* She was built in Romania to a German design. Slightly smaller than her predecessor, she displaced 620 tons and was armed with six 21in torpedo tubes plus a 4in gun and a 37mm gun. She was laid down in 1938 and completed in 1942.

Similar to the *Marsuinul,* the *Rechinul* was also built in Romania to a German design. A mine-laying submarine, she displaced 585 tons and was armed with four 21in torpedo tubes and had capacity for forty mines. She also entered service in 1942.

Five Italian midget submarines of the CB class CB1, 2, 3, 4 and 6 were transferred to Romania in September, 1943; all were subsequently scuttled in August, 1944.

Delfinul remained in service until 1957. *Marsuinul* and *Rechinul* were deleted in 1967, though all had been withdrawn from active service in 1961. Romania was then to be without a submarine arm for nineteen years.

In December, 1986, the Soviet Union transferred a *Kilo* Class submarine (SSK) to the Romanian flag. It is anticipated that a number of others of the same class will follow, though this depends entirely on funds being made available which at present seems unlikely.

SUBMARINE INSIGNIA

As far as can be ascertained Romania originally had no specialist submarine qualification badge. However, a series of war badges were created on 17 June, 1943. There were seven categories, one of which was for submarines. It was awarded for forty days' active service at sea but immediate awards could be made for actual combat or for being wounded.

The insignia, which was in metal, was very similar in design to the Italian submarine service badge. It consisted of a leaping dolphin (said to allude to the first Romanian submarine of that name) surrounded by a broad band of which the bottom part was in the form of a wreath. The word 'Svbmarine' was inscribed at the top of the band. The device was surmounted by the Royal Crown. It was worn in gilt by officers, silver for petty officers and a dull white metal for junior ratings.

After the Monarchy was overthrown (December, 1947) a new insignia made its appearance. It was quite different in design from the insignia worn by other countries. It was manufactured in metal and was in the shape of an eagle (facing the wearer's left) above two crossed swords. On the eagle's chest was an enamelled shield in red, on which was a double white cross atop three blue hills. The insignia was worn on the left side of the jacket, fixed by a screw fastening, and was gold for officers, silver for petty officers and a grey metal for junior ratings. It was said to measure 20mm x 13mm. Unusual in appearance for a submarine badge, especially as the central device closely resembles the national arms of Slovakia (the Apostolic Cross and representation of the Tatra Mountains). This may allude to some former connection between the two states or the design may 'just have been borrowed'. Nevertheless the details here came directly from the Romanian Naval Authorities. It is possible that the insignia may have been specifically authorized for service in miniature submarines which had a dual role for torpedo attack and for carriers of combat swimmers (frogmen). Further speculation on its authenticity cannot be ruled out. With the demise of the submarine service in 1967 the insignia ceased to be awarded. Official information received in 1993 stated that no special insignia exists for submariners.

A small white metal anodized aluminium badge appeared about 1994. It depicts a black *Kilo* Class submarine with an open-topped white metal wreath around the central part of the hull and sail, in the centre of which

ROMANIA

is the numeral '55' in red. At the base of the wreath are the national colours, blue, yellow and red, the whole being picked out in white metal. It measures 49mm x 28mm and has a very flimsy pin and hook fixing at the back.

Because of its metal and fixing it is unlikely to be a uniform item for submarine qualification and more likely to be a commemorative badge of some kind. Specialist insignia for a one-submarine fleet would be of a low priority.

Romanian War Badge created 1943 in gold for officers, silver for senior ratings and dull white metal for junior ratings. Lapsed with fall of monarchy in 1947.

(above) Romanian submarine insignia about 1994 probably a commemorative badge for wear on civilian clothes.

Romanian submarine service insignia, post-war to about 1961.

RUSSIA: MONARCHY

RUSSIAN SUBMARINE SERVICE

Experiments were carried out with a German-built submarine in the Baltic as early as 1854. In 1866 a submarine was built by an engineer named Alexandrovsky. It proved to be a failure as were some fifty four-man, hand-propelled, mine-laying submersibles that followed in 1878. Most were either cancelled or converted into mooring buoys.

The first Czarist submarine to actually enter service was the *Petr Kochka* completed at Kronstadt in 1902. She was built in sections so that she could be transported by rail to Port Arthur. Her displacement was a mere 20 tons but she could carry two small torpedoes. A second submarine, the *Delphin*, foundered at Kronstadt but was raised and used for training. Both boats were out of service before World War I commenced.

Between 1904 and 1905 a few small experimental submarines were deployed at Port Arthur and Vladivostok but failed to achieve any results against the Japanese. Several boats were then purchased from America, Germany and Italy. Just before World War I the *Tigr* class was laid down. These were the first Russian-designed submarines.

On the outbreak of war in 1914 Russia had thirty-seven submarines and nineteen under construction. Of the active boats fourteen were in the Baltic, eleven in the Black Sea and twelve were in the Siberian Flotilla based at Vladivostok. Pre-war boats were mostly Holland and American Lake types of between 150 and 200 tons and armed with two to four torpedo tubes. Among these was the world's first mine-laying submarine, the *Krab*. The majority were underpowered and poorly constructed, requiring constant repairs.

Six more classes were built during the war, including eighteen US-manufactured H Class assembled in Russian yards (of which three survived to serve in World War II). Altogether fifty-eight submarines served under the Russian flag during World War I; of these seven were discarded and eight were lost before October, 1917. Of the remainder twenty-four were lost during the Civil War, including four that escaped to Bizerta on the collapse of the White Cause. Thirteen were scuttled by the British to prevent them falling into Bolshevik hands. Shortly after the Civil War three submarines in the Baltic fleet and four in the Caspian Flotilla were deleted. The Czarist fleet had ceased to exist.

The performance of the Russian submarine fleet during World War I was not spectacular, though a few minor successes were achieved against German and neutral Swedish merchant ships in the Baltic. Its record in the Black Sea was much better, with Turkish transports being the main targets. At no time did it pose a serious threat to the German Navy.

RUSSIAN SUBMARINE INSIGNIA

The submarine distinguishing badge was an insignia only available to officers who had graduated from the Navy Department Submarine Course. It was authorized on 26 January, 1909, and was manufactured in silver metal measuring 43mm x 45mm. The design consisted of a fouled anchor over which, and facing to the wearer's left, was a submarine. Anchor and submarine were surrounded by the links of an anchor chain.

Imperial Russian insignia for Officers Submarine Class, Navy Department, 1909-17.

USSR
& POST-COMMUNIST RUSSIA

SOVIET SUBMARINE SERVICE

After the Revolution the Russian Navy was re-styled the Red Fleet. Few submarines remained from Czarist days and most of those that did were unserviceable. Only ten were left in the Baltic, five in the Black Sea and one in the Arctic.

It was not until 1928 that the first class of new submarines was laid down. This was the D Class of six vessels based on Italian design. These were followed by the L Class of twenty-five mine-laying submarines based on British design. The SHCH Class, originally of four boats but many more were to follow, made their first appearance in 1930.

It was evident that by now the Soviet Union was intent on making her submarine force the spearhead of her Navy. Between 1927 and 1939 twenty classes (and sub-classes) consisting of 281 submarines were laid down. In 1939, at the commencement of the Winter War with Finland, one hundred and eighty-five had been completed. This made it the world's largest submarine force. Despite having fifty-five submarines in the Baltic only six small merchant ships were sunk, of which two were neutral. Against this the Red Fleet lost six of its submarines.

In 1941, when Hitler attacked the Soviet Union, the Red Fleet had 218 submarines in commission and many more were in various stages of construction. Ninety-one were laid down during the war. However, only fifty-two of these were completed before the war ended. Of those that remained, most were destroyed on their slipway or abandoned. Twenty-two other submarines, including five pocket submarines, were acquired from abroad. Great Britain and America transferred five each and the Soviet seized two from Estonia, two from Latvia and eight from Romania.

The Stalin purges of 1937-8 decimated the officer corps, resulting in a lack of expertise to develop submarine tactics. This lack of expert leadership, despite much evidence of courage, accounted in some part for the poor performance of the Red Fleet submarines during World War II. Soviet figures at the end of the war claimed that their submarines had sunk a total of 417 enemy vessels. Allied estimates made the figure 136. Although 173 Soviet submarines survived the war at least 108 were lost.

In 1948 Stalin announced the first post-war building programme. It called for the construction of 1,200 submarines to be built at the rate of seventy-eight per year. This figure was later raised to one hundred per year. With the advent of nuclear propulsion a large proportion of this vast programme was cancelled. Five classes totalling 388 diesel/electric submarines were completed. These were the coastal submarines of the *Quebec* Class, the medium range submarines of the *Whiskey* and *Romeo* Classes and the long-range submarines of the *Zulu* and *Foxtrot* Classes (all SS).* Construction of submarines then split into three groups: attack submarines (SS), cruise missile submarines (SSG) and ballistic missile submarines (SSB).

The next generation of conventional attack submarines (SSK) were the eighteen boats of the *Tango* Class in 1973, followed in 1979 by the

---

*Note: NATO designators are used for class names with the exception of the *Severodvinsk* Class.

first of thirteen *Kilo* Class. Nuclear-powered attack submarines (SSN) made their appearance between 1959 and 1963 with the twelve vessels of the *November* Class. With a displacement of 4,200 tons and armed with eight 21in torpedo tubes, their primary task was to attack enemy surface shipping. The *Victor* Class (I, II, III) of forty-four SSNs followed between 1967 and 1978. Armed with six 21in torpedo tubes (and the IIIs were capable of firing the SS-N-15 anti-submarine missiles through their tubes) they were the first of the hunter-killers (anti-submarine submarines).

The revolutionary *Alpha* Class (SSN), initially of six boats, first appeared in 1970. They were the world's first submarines to be constructed from titanium, which not only returns a low magnetic signature, but also its great strength enables the submarines to dive to a depth of more than 3,000ft, twice that of Western submarines. Their high speed also enabled them to out-run all current Western A/S torpedoes. Two *Sierra* and one *Mike* Class (SSNs) entered service in 1983-4 armed with torpedoes and SS-N-21 (land attack) missiles and two *Sierra* IIs (SSN) commissioned in 1990-3. The *Akula* Class first appeared in 1984-5. Of advanced design, they have a dived tonnage of 8,000 tons and are armed with six 21in torpedo tubes and the SS-N-21 missile. This missile system can be fired through the torpedo tubes. A number of older ballistic missile submarines had also been converted to the attack role. The lead ship of a new class, the dual purpose SSN/SSGN *Severodvinsk* Class of three and possibly four more is due to enter service in 1998.

In the early 1950s experiments were carried out with submarine-mounted cruise missiles, a type of weapon that remains a Soviet monopoly. The first submarines to be so mounted were the *Whiskey* Class (SSG). In 1956 one boat was fitted with a single SS-N-3 (range 12 NM). In 1959 a further five were fitted with two SS-N-3A (range 250 NM). These elderly versions required the submarine to fire its missiles on the surface. In 1961 six *Whiskeys* were converted to carry four SS-N-3 which were enclosed within the control tower. The first purpose-built cruise (or guided) missile submarines (SSG) were the sixteen *Juliet* Class boats. They entered between 1961 and 1968. They had a displacement of 3,000 tons and were armed with four SS-N-3A missiles and six torpedo tubes.

All further cruise missile submarines were to be nuclear-propelled (SSGN). The first of these were the *Echo* Class. Five mark Is with six SS-N-3 and twenty-nine mark IIs with eight SS-N-3 were built. Like all Soviet SSGNs they were also armed with torpedo tubes. Then came the *Charlie* Is and IIs between 1967 and 1980. The eleven Is had eight SS-N-7 (range 35NM) and the six IIs had eight SS-N-9 (range 60 NM).

One *Papa* Class entered service in 1971 armed with ten SS-N-9. The latest submarines of this type are the *Oscar* Class I and II (SSGN) of which five had been built, the first entering service in 1980. Huge vessels of 12,500 and 13,400 tons (dived) they mount twenty-four SS-N-19 (range 295 NM). They also are armed with new large 22.6in torpedoes. A number of older Y Class SSBNs have been converted to a SSGN role.

Ballistic missiles were first fitted into submarines in 1958. Selected for this purpose were ten conventional submarines of the ZV Class. Each was fitted with two vertical launch tubes for SS-N-4 (range 300 NM) in the sail. The purpose-built *Golf* Class (SSB) followed between 1958 and 1962. Twenty-three altogether, the mark IIIs had six SS-N-8 (range 4,260 NM) and the single mark V had one SS-N-20 (range 4,540 NM). There were five groups in all but various submarines within the class were re-graded. Like all Soviet SSBNs, they were also armed with torpedoes.

Future vessels of this type were all nuclear-powered (SSBN). The first of these were the *Hotel* Class of eight. They were originally armed with six SS-N-4s. They were later upgraded to SS-N-5 and finally to SS-N-8. Next came the *Yankee* Class. Thirty-four were built between 1967 and 1974, of which thirteen were later converted to SSNs. Their missile armament consisted of sixteen SS-N-6 (range 1,300 NM later upgraded to 1,640 NM). This relatively short range made it necessary for them to transit great distances in order to arrive 'on station'. The *Deltas* (I, II, III, IV) that followed in 1972/84 all had long-range missiles which meant that they could remain in the relatively safe waters off their own coastline. The eighteen mark Is had twelve SS-N-8. The four mark IIs had sixteen SS-N-8, the fourteen mark IIIs had sixteen SS-N-18 (range 3,550 NM) and the four mark IVs had sixteen SS-N-23 (range 4,540 NM). Large boats, they displace between 8,300 and 11,000 tons.

The latest SSBNs to come into service are the *Typhoon* Class. Estimated to have a displacement of between 25,000 and 30,000 tons, they are the largest submarines ever built. Their missile armament consists of twenty SS-N-20 (range 4,540 NM). The first of a planned class of six entered service in 1983.

The Soviet Navy ceased to exist on the 1 January, 1992. On that date the Soviet Union was split into fifteen independent republics and assumed the name of the Commonwealth of Independent States. The armed forces were shared out, but the vast bulk of the former Red Fleet went to Russia. As far as is known this included all submarines.

The Russian submarine fleet as of 1996 consists of thirty-nine SSBNs, eighteen SSGNs, one SSG, fifty-two SSNs, forty-two SSKs and fifteen auxiliaries. Numerous older submarines have transferred to other navies, been laid up or have been scrapped.

Despite Russia's economic situation and the hugely rising costs in the construction and maintenance of keeping ships operational, Russia is continuing to build submarines at a yearly rate of one SSBN, one or two SSNs and two or three SSKs. It is estimated that by the end of the century there will be nearly sixty more submarines in service than those at present. The world should take note!

SUBMARINE INSIGNIA

Accurate information on the Soviet/Russian submarine insignia is extremely difficult to obtain. The reader is therefore warned that the following details have been based on the best available information, but lacks official Soviet sanction.

The first submarine badge was authorized in 1942 and was styled the badge for 'Submarine Commander'. This has been interpreted as the badge for commanding officers of submarines. This may be an oversimplification as between 1918 and 1943 all Soviet officers were collectively referred to as Commanders. Photographic evidence exists of officers who appear too junior to be in command wearing the badge. It is therefore still not clear who is entitled to wear it. It is awarded for meritorious service and achievement.

Originally the badge was manufactured in grey oxidised metal (perhaps due to wartime restrictions) but later models were made in bright silver. It depicts a conventional submarine with two deck guns facing the wearer's left. In the centre of the hull there is a red enamel star. It measures 68mm x 22mm and it has a screw fastening on the back. The securing nut is round and bears, in the Cyrillic alphabet, the inscription 'Forward to Victory, Moscow'. The badge comes in one size only and it is worn on the right breast. Recipients may continue to wear the insignia throughout their service careers. It is regarded in much the same light as a medal and it is awarded with due ceremony. Illustrations that appeared about 1965 show a slightly different design, the main difference being that the submarine has no deck guns. Little has been seen of this variation since that time.

In the early 1990s a gold version of the insignia appeared. This is said to be worn by highly ranking officers though illustrations show Admirals wearing the silver badge. The Soviet Navy has always had a gold and silver ranking system, denoting line or service; thus the colour may relate to a specific appointment. Otherwise gold-coloured badges should be treated with suspicion. A miniature, possibly unofficial, measuring 38mm x 13mm appeared about 1992.

Graduates of the Submarine Academy wear the usual diamond-shaped academy badge 45mm high. It has a red star with the Soviet coat-of-arms in its centre, below which, on a small plate, are the Cyrillic letters for 'VVMU' denoting the Submarine Service Naval Academy Plavania.

A series of seven proficiency badges known as Best Soldier (Sailor) Badges were instituted on 21 May, 1942. They were all the same basic design, being shield shape with oak leaves on either side. The top portions bore a white circlet, bearing a Cyrillic inscription, surrounding a hammer and sickle on a red field. At the base of the shield was an emblem denoting the speciality. In the case of the submarine service this was a small gold submarine. The badges measured 34mm x 38mm and were worn on the right breast. This series of insignia eventually totalled twenty-three specialities but only the one remained specifically for submariners. On 1 April, 1967, these badges were replaced by three new ones, one each for the Army, Navy and Air Force; thus submarine ratings lost their only distinctive emblem.

Officers and ratings can also qualify for Long Cruise Badges. These are made of coloured enamel metal badges and take various forms. The 1961 Long Cruise pattern depicts a submarine above an inscribed base and semi-wreath, above which is a Naval Ensign. The one for 1976 is shaped rather like a shield. It displays a Soviet Naval Ensign at the top, a nuclear submarine with a representation of a globe over an inscription in the centre and an anchor over waves at the bottom. These badges are worn on the right breast. As long cruises became more common such badges became less prolific.

Numerous submarine-related badges also exist. These are for commemorative events or anniversaries or are for long and special service. Most are not intended for wear on uniform; those that are usually (but not always) have a screw fixing on the back.

No changes in submarine insignia has occurred since the collapse of communism. It is assumed that the existing insignia will continue to be worn, though other types may be added.

RUSSIA

Soviet Union, submarine qualification insignia for commanding officers.

Unofficial in gold.

Soviet Union, ratings submarine proficiency badge 1942-57.

Soviet Union Submarine Long Cruise Badge 1961.

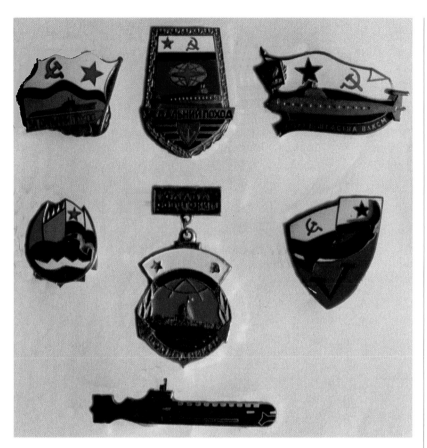

Soviet Union, selection of commemorative and similar insignia not meant for wear on uniforms.

Soviet Union Submarine Long Cruise Badge 1976.

SAUDI ARABIA

SUBMARINE SERVICE

Persistent rumours have indicated that Saudi Arabia has been consider-
ing the purchase of patrol submarines (SSK). Saudi naval officers have
received training in the navies of France and Pakistan, which points to
the French *Agosta* Class as being front-runners. The acquiring of such
submarines is, however, a low priority. It is more likely that smaller submarines, probably suited for commando infiltration (SDV), will enter
service first.

SUBMARINE INSIGNIA

Thought to be quite unofficial, a small number of badges were contracted for about 1981 to a United States insignia manufacturer who
sub-contracted the order to a small company that did casting work. The
casting company reportedly went out of business in 1983 and efforts to
track down the moulds proved unsuccessful.

The insignia depicted a central motif of unfouled anchor about which
were crossed scimitars and above that a palm tree and crossed flags, all
surmounted by a royal crown. Either side were inward-facing dolphins
similar in design to those depicted on USN submarine badges. Between
the crown and the dolphin's heads, on each side, were three bolts of
lightning.

The badges were made in heavy metal casting with clutchback fasteners. The finish was in bright gold but with a silver anchor. It measured
75mm x 43mm and there was a miniature version. It is likely that these
badges were intended for the crews of midget submarines and SDVs
who would also be combat swimmers.

*Saudi Arabian submarine
insignia, probably for SDV
crews and may be unofficial.*

SINGAPORE

SUBMARINE SERVICE
Singapore purchased the 28-year-old Swedish submarine *Sjöbjörnen* of the *Sjöormen* Class (SSK) in October, 1995. She is expected to be delivered in the second half of 1997. She is more than twice the size of the projected German Type 206 Class which are thought to be front-runners for the new submarine service. This submarine will be used as a training ship to provide personnel for from two to four smaller submarines to follow. Her large size will provide accommodation for trainees and space for fitting trial equipment for tropical conditions. The new submarines are not expected to be ordered before 1998/9.

SUBMARINE INSIGNIA
No details are presently available.

SOUTH AFRICA

SUBMARINE SERVICE
Only three submarines have served in the South African Navy. They are the French-built *Daphne* Class, *Maria Van Riebeeck*, *Emily Hobhouse* and *Johanna Van Der Merwe*. The first was commissioned in 1970 and the other two in 1971.

Two French *Agosta* Class were ordered in 1975. A subsequent United Nations ban on the sale of armaments to South Africa resulted in them being sold, instead, to Pakistan.

The three submarines in service have all been modernized to enable them to continue in service until 2005.

SUBMARINE INSIGNIA
On the formation of the submarine arm, a submarine service badge was authorized. It took the form of a simplistic representation of a modern submarine in gilt metal facing the wearer's left. The device measured 65mm x 16mm and was the same for all ranks. It was first presented on 16 January, 1970.

In 1974 the design was changed. This followed the introduction into the Navy of four specialist badges for all sea-going personnel. The categories were 'independent ships', 'strike craft', 'mine counter measures' and 'submarines'. All were produced in metal and were of a similar basic design.

The submarine badge depicts a *Daphne* Class submarine in gold colour facing the wearer's left. Behind the submarine is an upright trident and wreath in silver colour. The device is worn on the right mid-breast and is secured by a pair of clutch fasteners. The dimensions are 58mm x 40mm.

The qualifications required are:
1 be medically fit for submarine service,
2 successfully complete submarine course part I,
3 be up-to-date with submarine escape training,
4 have served in a submarine at sea for at least forty-five days,
5 complete applicable qualifying task book,
6 be recommended by commanding officers as being competent and suitable to fill a post on board commensurate with rank and
7 display the required ability, sense of responsibility and submarine awareness.

The insignia may be worn throughout the recipient's service. A miniature version is said to exist but this may not be official. A printed cloth version is available for the all-weather working uniform.

South African submarine qualification insignia, all ranks.
Top: 1970-4.
Bottom: from 1974.

SPAIN

SUBMARINE SERVICE

The Spanish submarine service began in 1915 with the ordering from the United States of a 488 ton submarine of the Holland type. She was named *Isaac Peral* and was armed with four torpedo tubes and a 3in QF gun. Three more submarines were laid down in 1917 in Italian yards and were delivered between 1916 and 1920. Much smaller than their predecessor, they displaced 260 tons and had an armament of two 18in torpedo tubes and a 3 pdr gun.

Between 1923 and 1925 six more submarines were constructed in Italy. They formed the C Class, displaced 915 tons and were fitted with six 21in torpedo tubes and one 4.7in gun. Two were sunk during the Spanish Civil War, though one was subsequently raised and refitted. During the Civil War four Italian submarines served with the Spanish Nationalist Forces. For details see the section on Italy.

The D Class, Spanish-built, consisting of three submarines, entered service between 1941 and 1943. They displaced 1,050 tons and were armed with six 21in torpedo tubes, a 4.7in gun and two machine guns. The German U 573 which had been interned in Spain in 1942 was purchased in 1943 and was renamed G7.

In 1959, after most of the earlier boats had been paid off, the United States transferred the *Balao* Class submarine (SS) USS *Kraken* to Spain.

In 1957 and 1958 Spain added two classes of midget submarines to her Navy. The first class of two boats, designated the *Foca* Class, displaced 16 tons, were armed with two 21in torpedo tubes and had a crew of three. Both were deleted in 1971. The second class, also of two boats, designated the *Tiburnon* Class, displaced 78 tons and had a similar armament and were manned by a crew of five. Both were disposed of in 1977.

By 1971 the remaining D Class and the ex-German U-boat had been broken up. The United States transferred four more submarines between 1971 and 1974. These were the USS *Ronquil*, *Picuda*, *Bang* and *Jallao* of the *Guppy* IIA Class (SS).

More modern purpose-built submarines were built in Spain between 1968 and 1974. Designated the S60 *Delfin* Class they were based on the French *Daphne* Class and were built under licence. Four more French-designed submarines were constructed in Spain between 1977 and 1984. These were of the French *Agosta* Class and were given the Spanish designation of S70 *Galerna* Class.

The present (1996) Spanish Submarine Arm consists of these last two

SPAIN

classes. The next generation of submarines which have been designated S80 *Scorpene* Class are being developed in conjunction with France. Of about 2,000 tons displacement, construction is scheduled to commence in 1999.

SUBMARINE INSIGNIA

The Spanish Navy first authorized a submarine qualification badge on 5 September, 1919. It depicted a stylized version of a Holland type submarine with a single deck gun. It faced the wearer's left and was surmounted by a Royal Crown. It was manufactured in both gold wire embroidery and in gold-coloured metal. The metal version had a brooch fixing and was intended for wear on the white uniform. A red enamel oval was situated in the centre of the hull and below the conning tower for all personnel serving in or having served in submarines. For cadets at the Submarine School and for personnel who had completed their training but had not been assigned to submarines, the oval was in blue enamel. In the case of the metal badge the crown was detached; consequently many survive without the crown.

Admiralty order dated 30 March, 1934, further defined the insignia and gave its dimensions as 85mm wide, though slightly narrower examples may be found. No mention was made regarding the Royal Crown. Despite the fact that King Alfonso XIII was forced to leave the country in April, 1931, and a republic was proclaimed, the King refused to abdicate. It was not until 1941 that he renounced his rights in favour of his son Don Juan. This may explain why the crown may have been retained.

New orders on 1 October, 1934, dropped the mention of the blue oval, but as it was again mentioned in later orders this is not thought to be significant, though at this stage reports suggest that the same design but with a mural crown had the coloured stone replaced by a gold-coloured anchor on a red oval background. This was said to have been worn from 1931 to 1939.

During The Spanish Civil War (18 July, 1936 to 29 March, 1939) submarine personnel on the Nationalist side began to change the badge to a different one, also with a crown, but depicting a *Cavallini* Class submarine with two deck guns. This measured 66mm x 22mm and much later an unofficial miniature was produced measuring 34mm x 12mm. On 10 June, 1939, the crown was replaced by a coronet as shown on the then Spanish coat-of-arms. This was prescribed by Generalissimo Franco in a letter to the Under-Secretary of the Admiralty on 27 May, 1938.

The regulations were again altered on 10 January, 1941; these orders elaborated on the wearing of the submarine insignia by ratings. For seamen the badge without the coronet but including a red disc (rather than the previous oval shape) was to be embroidered on a rectangular piece of dark blue cloth measuring 67mm x 34mm. This insignia was to be worn 148mm below the shoulder seam on the right upper arm. For petty officers the same badge but with the coronet was to be sewn on the right breast, the only one to be worn there. This badge was of a different design being somewhat similar to the submarine used on the 1919 insignia but with upswept bows.

Admiralty Order of 14 January, 1957, reiterated previous regulations, but stated that the badge depicting the red disc could continue to be worn by those who had left the submarine service because of age or injury.

Admiralty Order dated 28 December, 1962, stated that any badge differing from the regulations would be exchanged by the Submarine School. This may explain the proliferation of insignia showing variations in design.

The next significant change came on 30 July, 1975, when all qualified personnel were to wear the badge with a red translucent circular stone imbedded in the centre of the hull. Cadets were to wear a similar stone in green and personnel associated with the submarine service but not actually serving at sea, but with a minimum of two years service, were to wear the stone in black. These associated personnel included maintenance engineers, supply personnel, chaplains and medical personnel, plus various smaller categories serving ashore.

The regulations of 25 October, 1978, reintroduced the Royal Crown (King Juan Carlos acceded to the throne on 22 November, 1975). It gave the dimensions of the new badge as 65mm x 22mm. Flag officers, officers, petty officers and re-enlisted leading seamen (*cabos primeros*) were to wear the insignia on the right breast and junior ratings were to wear it on the right upper sleeve. The metal badge had a brooch fixing. An unofficial miniature measuring 34mm x 14mm was later produced.

Finally the Admiralty Order dated 29 July, 1986, altered the design of the insignia reverting to the original style of 1919 but with the following changes: the Royal Crown now included red cushions (in the metal version it was attached to the periscopes), the overall dimensions were reduced to 70mm x 30mm (though some variations measure 68mm x 30mm), and the translucent stones retain their circular shape. In future these stones were to be red for officers and green for ratings, the black stone for associated personnel was done away with altogether, leaving only the submarine device. The metal version was fixed to the uniform with three clutch fasteners. There is no official miniature but doubtless an unofficial one will appear.

Junior ratings in the submarine service can further be distinguished by the name or number of their submarine on their cap ribbon. Those attached to the Submarine School bear the inscription 'SUB-MARINOS'.

Spanish submarine qualification insignia 1919-38.

Spanish submarine qualification insignia 1919-38 (crown missing).

Spanish submarine qualification insignia for officers and senior ratings 1941-78. Red stone for submarine officers and black stone for associated officers. During most of this period junior ratings wore the same insignia as submarine officers but without the coronet.

Spanish submarine qualification insignia worn by petty officers 1941-78, original version.

Spanish submarine qualification insignia worn by junior ratings on right sleeve 1941-78, original version.

Spanish submarine qualification insignia first pattern, monarchy, (stone missing) 1978-86, and second pattern, monarchy, with red stone for officers, from 1986.

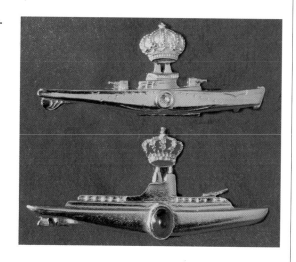

Spanish submarine qualification insignia 1978-86 with red stone for officers and black stone for attached personnel (doctors, supply officers and chaplains, etc). This design also appears with a slightly smaller crown and a cable cutter on the bow.

Spanish submarine qualification insignia from 1986 in gold wire embroidery.

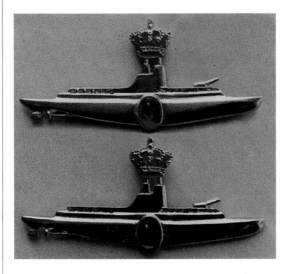

Spanish submarine qualification insignia, second pattern, for monarchy, with red stone for officers and green stone for junior ratings, from 1986.

Sweden

Submarine Service

Traditionally Sweden has built her own warships, and submarines, for the main part, were no exception. The first submersible came into service in 1904. Named *Hajen*, it was based on the Holland type, displaced 107 tons and was fitted with one 18in torpedo tube. She was followed by the Laurenti type *Hvalen* in 1909. Slightly larger, she displaced 180 tons and had double the armament. She was the sole exception to tradition, being Italian-built. Between 1910 and 1911 a class of five, numbered 3 to 7 (instead of being named) were constructed. Their displacement and armament was the same as their Italian-built predecessor.

During World War I three classes, consisting of seven submarines, were completed (*Tumlaren, Delfinen* and *Abboren* Classes). Some of these remained in service until the mid-1970s. The *Haljen* Class of 300 tons, three in number, followed in 1920. Between 1920 and 1923 four more submarines designated the *Bavern* Class were constructed. They displaced 500 tons and were armed with four 20.8in torpedo tubes, one 6 pdr gun and one machine gun. One of this class, the *Valen*, was fitted out as a mine-layer.

The *Draken* Class of three boats entered service between 1924 and 1929. They displaced 700 tons and were armed with four 21in torpedo tubes and a 3in gun. The *Ulven* of this class was sunk by a mine in 1943. The three submarines of the *Delfinen* Class, constructed between 1934 and 1935 were of 540 tons and were armed with four 21in torpedo tubes, a single 57mm AA gun and were fitted as mine-layers.

Laid down just before World War II the *Sjölejonet* Class of nine vessels was completed during that war. They were of 580 tons and were fitted with six 21in torpedo tubes, two 40mm AA guns and two machine guns. They were the first fully Swedish designed submarines. War construction produced nine coastal submarines of the U Class. Numbered U1 to U9 they displaced 367 tons and were armed with four 21in torpedo tubes and a 20mm AA gun.

Post-war development began in 1964 with the launching of the first submarine of the six *Hajen* Class. These vessels were 790 tons displacement and mounted four 21in torpedo tubes and one 20mm AA gun. The former British X Class midget submarine HMS *Stickleback* was purchased in 1968 and remained in service until the early 1970s. The six-vessel *Draken* Class (Type A II) (SS) of 835 tons with four 21in torpedo tubes were launched between 1960 and 1961.

The first 'tear drop' submarines were launched between 1967 and 1968. Designated the *Sjöormen* Class (Type A 12) (SSK), they displace 1,125 tons and are armed with four 21in and two 15.75in torpedo tubes. Returning to a more conventional appearance, the *Nacken* Class (Type A 14) (SSK) were launched in 1978-9. This class of three units of 1,015 tons surface displacement is armed with six 21in torpedo tubes and two 15.75in torpedo tubes, plus a minelaying capability. In 1978 an underwater rescue vehicle was launched and in 1985 two Yugoslav Chariot Type swimmer vehicles were purchased designated R1 and R2. R1 was deleted in 1990. A midget submarine, *Spiggen II*, displacing 14 tons dived, was launched in 1990.

The *Vastergötland* (Type A 17) Class (SSK) was constructed between 1983 and 1988. The class numbers four boats displacing 1,070 tons and armed with six 21in and three 15.75in torpedo tubes. They also have the

SWEDEN

capacity to carry twenty-two mines. A new class designated *Gotland* (Type A19) (SSK) is to be commissioned between 1996 and 1997. They will displace 1,240 tons and will eventually replace the *Sjöormen* Class.

Swedish submarine design, by Kockums of Malmo, has reached a high level which has led to a high export trade.

The submarine force at spring 1996 consisted of four *Vastergötland* Class (SSK), three *Nacken* Class (SSK), four *Sjöormen* Class (SSK) and one midget (*Spiggen II*) used as ASW training target.

SUBMARINE INSIGNIA

The first Swedish submarine badge appeared in 1956. It was quite unofficial but, despite the threat of arrest by the military police, it was worn with much pride by most submariners. The badge was made in gold-coloured metal measuring 66mm x 22mm and it had a brooch fixing. The design was of a Neptune's trident, behind which was the sail (or conning tower) of an on-coming partially submerged submarine flanked by two waves.

In January, 1978, the Swedish Navy authorized an official insignia. It is the same for all ranks and is embroidered in gold on dark blue cloth. The design depicts a trident within a shield surmounted by a Royal Crown. Guarding the central motif on either side is an outward-facing shark (alluding to Sweden's first submarine *Hajen*, named after the Swedish for shark). The device, including background, measures 82mm x 30mm.

In 1986 a gold-coloured metal version was authorized for wear on shirts and sweaters. It was sponsored by the Swedish submarine yard Kockums after being initially vetoed by the Swedish Naval Command. It received their consent on condition that it would not be made available to the general public. It measures 73mm x 23mm and can have clutch or screw fastenings. Each badge is numbered on the reverse. Submariners are issued with one each. Replacements can only be obtained by producing genuine evidence that the original has been lost.

The submarine insignia is worn on the right side of the uniform above the breast pocket by all qualified personnel. The qualifications for wear are: for officers to complete six months' service in a submarine after graduating from the qualifying course, for conscripts to have completed their military service with sufficient grades to be part of a wartime submarine crew. Swedish Naval conscripts serve 10 to 17½ months, then return at six-year intervals for 18 to 40 days refresher periods until the age of 47.

Swedish sailors serving in submarines wear the name of their vessel on the cap ribbon. Branch badges are surmounted by the letter U.

Swedish unofficial submarine qualification insignia made in 1956 and worn until the 1960s.

Swedish official submarine insignia in gold wire embroidery 1978, all ranks.

Swedish submarine qualification insignia in metal, all ranks 1986.

SYRIA

SUBMARINE SERVICE

Three elderly ex-Soviet *Romeo* Class submarines (SS) were transferred to the Syrian flag in 1986. A year earlier an even older *Whiskey* Class submarine (SS) was acquired. It was relegated to harbour service and provided battery-charging facilities for the three *Romeo* Class units. Two *Romeos* were deleted in 1993-4 leaving only one in service.

Two R1 and two R2 *Mala* Class SDVs were acquired from Yugoslavia in the early 1980s. Their present status is unknown.

SUBMARINE INSIGNIA

Official sources (as of 26 April, 1989) confirm that no specialist submarine insignia exists.

TAIWAN

SUBMARINE SERVICE

The first submarines to serve in what is termed the 'Republic of China Navy' were two ex-American *Tench* Class (SS) modernized under the *Guppy* II programme. These are *Haih Shih* (ex-USS *Cutlass*) and *Haih Pao* (Ex-USS *Tusk*). Launched in 1944/5, both were transferred to Taiwan in 1973.

In 1984 a German-built midget research submarine was accepted into service. Forming the *Hai Lung* Class (SSK), *Hai Lung* and *Hai Hu* were built in the Netherlands. Both were laid down in 1982, launched in 1986 and commissioned in 1987/8. They are improved versions of the Dutch *Zwaardvis* Class, displace 1,870 tons and are armed with four 21in torpedo tubes. All these submarines remain in service today (1996). Plans to acquire new submarines have been thwarted because of protests from mainland China.

SUBMARINE INSIGNIA

The submarine insignia qualification badge was authorized on 10 January, 1977. It is the same design for all ranks. However, officers wear the device in gold, senior ratings wear it in silver and junior ratings wear it in grey metal. It comes in one size only and measures 70mm x 20mm. It is secured by a pair of clutch fasteners on the reverse.

The pattern consists of the national emblem in silver and blue enamel over a bow view of a modern 'tear drop' submarine flanked by dolphins. It bears a close resemblance to the submarine insignia of the US Navy.

The two dolphins on either side of the central motif symbolize the submarine fleet's responsibility of safeguarding the nation's territorial waters. The cross-shaped command tower (sail) represents the four codes of the submarine fleet: loyalty and boldness, absolute obedience, enthusiasm and initiative, and alertness and calmness.

The device is worn in the centre of the upper left pocket, above medal ribbons, if they are worn. There is also an unofficial miniature badge measuring 38mm x 11mm with two clutch fasteners.

For officers and petty officers the qualifications for wear are to have graduated from a submarine qualification course either at home or abroad and then to have been assigned to a submarine. Junior ratings have a less stringent requirement.

*Taiwan (Republic of China)
submarine qualification
insignia. Gold for officers
and silver for senior ratings.*

THAILAND

SUBMARINE SERVICE

Thailand's first submarines were four Japanese-built boats acquired between 1936 and 1937. They displaced 370 tons and were armed with five 21in torpedo tubes and one machine gun. Named *Majchanu, Plaichumpol, Sinsamut* and *Wirun,* they served until 1961 and were then decommissioned.

Since then the Royal Thai Navy has had no submarines. Plans to purchase submarines from Sweden and China in the late eighties were dropped due to financial restrictions.

At the beginning of 1995 the Thai Cabinet approved funds for the acquisition of three advanced submarines. These are likely to be built in Sweden, Germany or the Netherlands, though Russia and France have also shown an interest. A decision is likely to be made in the near future.

SUBMARINE INSIGNIA

There is some controversy concerning Thai submarine insignia. According to official sources no official submarine qualification device ever existed. An unofficial badge was, however, allowed to be worn by regular submarine officers and ratings on special occasions.

The insignia was the same for all ranks and was worn pinned to the right breast. It was manufactured in alloy and enamel and depicted a blue submarine, facing the wearer's left, surrounded by a 'Victory' wreath with seven white blossoms (*chaiya-pruek*). A small anchor was linked to the lower part of the submarine's bow. It was locally manufactured and was said to be worn between about 1937 and 1961.

Another badge often mistaken for a submarine badge is that of the combat swimmer. It consists of a central shield bearing the national colours red, white, blue, white and red, behind is a silver fouled anchor. Leaping sharks in silver on a gold representation of waves face the central motif on either side. These come in several sizes and variations and are also produced in cloth. The design is similar in nature to many other countries' submarine insignia and is included here to avoid confusion.

Unofficial submarine qualification insignia about 1937.

Thai combat swimmers insignia. Frequently mistaken for submarine insignia.

TURKEY

SUBMARINE SERVICE

During World War I the Turks, with German help, unsuccessfully attempted to refit two derelict Nordenfeldt submarines of 1889 vintage. It was not until 1928 that the first submarines actually entered service. These were the Dutch-built *Birinc Inônü* and the *Ikinci Inônö*. They displaced 506 tons and were armed with six 17.7in torpedo tubes and one 37mm gun. They were followed in 1931 by the Italian-built *Dumlupinar* of 830 tons and the submarine mine-layer *Sakarya* of 950 tons. Between 1935 and 1937 Germany built three submarines for Turkey. Named *Saldiray*, *Yildiray* and *Gür*, the first two displaced 934 tons and the third 760 tons.

It was not until the late 1940s that further submarines were added.

During that period and the early 1950s the United States transferred eight *Balao* Class (SS) to Turkey, and Great Britain transferred three P Class (SS). In the next few years various further *Balao* Class were exchanged for more modern variants. The most serving at any one time was ten.

In the early 1970s the *Balao*s were replaced by two ex-US *Guppy III*s (SS), seven ex-US *Guppy IIA*s (SS) and one *Guppy IA* (SS). These were further supplemented by two ex-*Tang* Class (SS) in 1980-3 for a five-year loan period.

A class of six new submarines entered service between 1975 and 1988. These are of the West Germany 209 Class (Type 1200). Known in Turkey as the *Atilay* Class (SSK), the first three were built in Kiel and the second three in Gölcük (Turkey). A further four are planned. These will be Type 1400 of the same class (SSK).

At the time of writing there are seventeen submarines in commission and three older submarines being used as shore accommodation hulks and power generating plants.

SUBMARINE INSIGNIA

On 24 September, 1926, the Turkish Navy announced that a submarine insignia would be authorized. This specialist badge came into being in 1928. For officers the device was manufactured in stainless cast brass and measured 56mm x 52mm. It consisted of a thick gold-coloured wreath of oak leaves on the right (representing war) and olive leaves on the left (representing peace). The wreath was tied together at the bottom with a ribbon and closed at the top with a star and crescent. Overlaid on the wreath was a representation of a submarine in black enamel outlined in silver and facing the wearer's left. This design, with slight modification, remains today. It is worn at the intersection of a centre line drawn from the left upper pocket and a line from the second button from the top of the jacket. There is also a miniature variation for use on mess dress. The miniature measures 18mm x 18mm and is of solid manufacture, whereas the standard device is voided within the wreath.

Career petty officers and conscripts, in the same year, were authorized to wear a solid brass oval device. This consisted of a similar wreath, ribbon and star and crescent to the officers badge but in the centre there was a submarine facing the wearer's right, behind which was a rising sun and above this were the letters 'TC'.

In 1935 the device ceased to be worn by junior ratings who were then authorized to wear a cloth insignia depicting a submarine facing either left or right. This device remains in use to this day and is normally

TURKEY

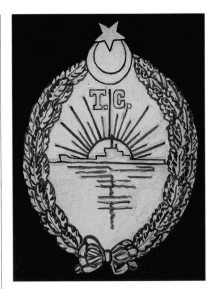

Turkish submarine qualification insignia
worn by petty officers 1956-9.

Turkish submarine qualification insignia for
petty officers and conscripts 1928-31.

Turkish submarine qualification insignia for
petty officers 1959-64.

Turkish submarine qualification insignia.
Large for officers and small for petty
officers. Worn from 1977 (though officers
wore a similar design from 1926).

Turkish submarine qualification insignia for
petty officers 1964-77. This same badge was
produced, probably erroneously, with the
submarine facing in the opposite direction.

worn on the left sleeve below other specialist and rank insignia. For professional ratings the device is manufactured in yellow on blue or white (depending on the uniform) and for conscripts, red on blue or white.

In 1956 career petty officers were granted a metal badge depicting a submarine facing the wearer's right, behind which was an oval rope device with a simple bow and a star and crescent at the top. In 1959 the device was altered so that the submarine faced the wearer's left and the bow became more elaborate.

The device was again altered in 1964 with the bow changing design slightly and the rope behind the submarine becoming more circular. It measures 55mm x 50mm and had a vertical brooch fastening. These early metal badges were rather crudely cast. A gold wire embroidered version also appeared. The wreath was slightly different, being more 'leafy' in appearance, with two buds at the base. It measured 52mm x 65mm.

In 1977 career petty officers were granted the right to wear the same insignia as that worn by officers, but to measure 26mm x 25mm. These new badges were much more fashionable and, in line with those worn by officers, were well made.

Dimensions and details of all insignia can vary considerably. Similar to the submarine badge is Frogman/Charioteer Badge. The submarine is replaced by a two-man chariot (torpedo-like craft with two frogmen sitting astride) in black or black edged in gold, facing the wearer's right.

Turkish submarine qualification insignia for junior ratings in cloth. Normally worn on right sleeve (in this case coxswain and electrician).

UKRAINE

The new Ukranian Navy seeks to acquire some former Soviet submarines, but no details of them or of any specific insignia are currently (1996) available.

UNITED KINGDOM

SUBMARINE SERVICE

The Royal Navy's submarine arm was born against a background of resentment and criticism. Most senior officers considered the submarine to be 'underhand and damned un-English'. Thus the Royal Navy reluctantly entered the submarine era rather later than did most other modern Navies. Originally submarines were termed 'submarine torpedo boats', hence they are usually referred to as 'boats'.

The first submarine to be launched was HM *Submarine No. 1* in October, 1901. She was a Holland VI boat, built under licence by Vickers Sons and Maxim. Her displacement was 120 tons and she was armed with a single torpedo tube. Four near sisters were constructed shortly afterwards. Boat *No. 1* was lost in 1913 while on tow to the breakers. Eventually raised in 1982, she is now preserved outside the submarine museum at HMS *Dolphin*, Gosport.

Having once started in the submarine field, construction began in earnest. By the start of World War I the Royal Navy possessed eighty-two submarines with twenty-two building. They were deployed world-wide with flotillas based in the Mediterranean, Gibraltar and China, plus nine flotillas in home waters.

After the original Hollands the first class to be constructed was the A Class of thirteen submarines built in 1904. They displaced between 120 and 200 tons and mounted two bow torpedo tubes. The B Class, of eleven 285 ton boats, followed in 1904-6 and the C Class of thirty-eight larger boats followed in 1906-10. The D Class of 1908-11, displacing 550 tons and armed with three torpedo tubes, were the first British submarines to mount a deck gun and be equipped with W/T. They were also the first to use diesel fuel rather than petrol.

The E Class of fifty-five boats were completed between 1913 and 1917. This type displaced 660 tons and six were the first British submarines to be fitted for mine-laying. War construction produced 118 boats in eleven main classes. Of note were the highly successful US-designed

H Class of which thirty were built during the war (followed by fourteen between 1918 and 1920). The first ten were built at Vickers in Montreal and the next eight were built at the Fore River Yard in the USA. Eight of these US-Built boats were impounded until America's entry into the war. Britain then transferred six to Chile in payment for Chilean ships building in British Yards and taken over by the Royal Navy. The remainder, referred to as the H21 type, were British-built. Some continued in service to be operational during World War II.

In 1916 the first steam-powered submarine, HMS *Swordfish*, was completed. She was followed by the notorious steam-powered fleet submarines of the K Class. Designed to accompany the battle fleet, their steam turbines gave them a surface speed of 24 knots. Originally flush-decked, bulbous clipper bows were later added to improve sea-worthiness. Each had two funnels which had to be lowered before submerging. Five of the class of seventeen were lost in accidents; thereafter steam propulsion was abandoned in submarines.

In April ,1916, E22 flew off two small sea-planes from a ramp fitted on the stern, the first British submarine to launch an aircraft.

The L Class of 1917-18, a development of the E Class, was perhaps the most effective war-built design. A number survived to participate in World War II. The M Class of 1918 were designed as submarine monitors and mounted a 12in gun. It had to be loaded on the surface but could be fired when all but the muzzle was submerged. After the war M2 had its 21in gun replaced by a hangar and aircraft.

At the conclusion of World War I 105 U-Boats were surrendered to the Royal Navy. At least three later flew the White Ensign.

With minor exceptions, Royal Navy submarines did not receive names until 1926. Up to that time they simply bore a number prefixed by the class letter. Shortly after the outbreak of war in 1939 the numbering system was restored, only to revert to naming in 1943.

Submarine production slackened after World War I. Experiments were made in the 1920s with submarine cruisers. The X-1 launched in 1923 was the largest submarine ever built for the Royal Navy until the nuclear-powered submarines of the 1960s. She displaced 3,050 tons and was armed with four 5.2in guns in two turrets, four machine guns and six 21in torpedo tubes. She was the only post-war submarine to be scrapped before 1939.

As war clouds gathered, submarine production once again picked up. By 1939 peacetime construction had added another nine classes to the fleet. When war commenced there were sixty-five submarines in service, of which thirteen were veterans of World War I building programmes.

War construction resulted in the production of 182 submarines; in addition seventeen were acquired from abroad. Of this last category: nine were ex-US, four were ex-Turkish, three were ex-Italian and one was ex-German. War construction was in three main classes: S, T and U. The later A Class was designed for use in the Pacific War, but hostilities ended before any entered service. Thirty-one midget submarines and numerous two-man chariots and a few one-man submarines designated Welmans had also been constructed. At the end of the war some one hundred and twelve enemy submarines, including midget craft, were surrendered to the Royal Navy. Eighty-five British submarines had been lost.

Post-war construction saw the completion of the A Class of fourteen and the launching of the *Explorer* Class of two unarmed experimental high-speed hydrogen-peroxide-powered submarines. At the same time four midget submarines (X Craft) were built, one of which was transferred to Sweden in 1958. By the 1960s both the experimental boats and the X Craft had been deleted.

The first post-war class of conventional patrol submarines (SS) were the eight boats of the *Porpoise* Class, followed by the launching between 1957 and 1964 of the similar *Oberon* Class (SS later SSK), of thirteen boats.

Britain's first nuclear-powered submarine was HMS *Dreadnought*, launched in 1960 and powered by a US reactor. She was a nuclear attack submarine (SSN), otherwise known as a hunter-killer (anti-submarine submarine). She displaced 3,500 tons and was armed with six 21in torpedo tubes. Her active life continued until 1986.

The first all-British nuclear attack submarines were the five vessels of the *Valiant/Churchill* Class (SSN). Launched in 1966-7, they displaced 4,000 tons and were armed with six 21in torpedo tubes, which could also launch Sub-Harpoon missiles. By 1994 all had been paid off.

The *Resolution* Class of four SSBNs, launched 1964-5, became Britain's Strategic Nuclear Deterrent Force when they came into service in the late sixties. They displaced 7,600 tons and were armed with sixteen Polaris A3 missiles and six 21in torpedo tubes.

The *Swiftsure* Class SSNs were launched between 1971 and 1979. There were five in the class, which displaced 4,000 tons, and were armed with five 21in torpedo tubes, which could also launch Sub-Harpoon missiles. The *Trafalgar* Class SSNs followed in the 1980s. Slightly larger than the *Swiftsure*s, they displaced 4,200 tons but had a similar armament. The initial class totalled seven boats. A second batch of five will be constructed to replace the *Swiftsure*s.

Returning to conventionally powered submarines (SSK), the *Up-*

holder Class (Type 2400) was ordered. Proposed as a class of ten, the first, HMS *Upholder*, was launched in 1986 and commissioned a year later. Three others followed, then further production was cancelled. These submarines displaced 2,400 tons (dived) and were given an armament of six 21in torpedo tubes which could also launch Sub-Harpoon SSM.

To update the United Kingdom's Strategic Nuclear Deterrent Force, a new generation of four SSBNs was initiated. Designated the *Vanguard* Class (SSBN), they are Britain's biggest ever submarines. They have a dived displacement of 16,000 tons and are armed with sixteen Trident D5 SLBMs, plus four 21in torpedo tubes. The first of the class was laid down in 1986 and commissioned in 1993, the second commissioned in 1995; the rest should follow into service by 1999.

Following the political upheavals in Eastern Europe in the early 1990s and the resultant proposed defence cuts, reductions were made. HMS *Revenge* (SSBN) was deleted in 1992 and her sister *Resolution* was deleted in 1994; the remainder of the class will be phased out and be replaced by the *Vanguard* Class. All four of the *Upholder* Class were paid off by June, 1994, the last conventionally powered submarines to serve in the Royal Navy.

At the time of writing (1996) the Royal Navy submarine fleet, consists of two *Vanguard* Class (SSBN), seven *Trafalgar* Class (SSNs) and five *Swiftsure* Class (SSNs).

SUBMARINE INSIGNIA

The first submarine distinguishing badge was a sub-speciality insignia for ratings only and made a brief appearance between 1958 and 1964. Irreverently referred to as the 'pregnant sausage' or 'sausage on a stick'. It proved unpopular and few were actually worn. It depicted a Holland type submarine facing its wearer's front (or to the left when observed) and was embroidered in gold on blue cloth, red on blue cloth and blue on white cloth. The dimensions were 70mm x 35mm. The dress regulations of the period stated it was to be worn on the right sleeve, by chief petty officers 1¼in above the centre button and by all other ratings 1½in above the cuff. Some official sources state that the insignia were never issued. This is true; they were never issued, but as their wear was optional naval stores did have them in stock and they were available for private purchase. This may explain why so few were actually worn.

Some sources claim that unofficial submarine badges were worn in World War I. This is entirely unfounded and quite misleading.

Inspired by the submarine badge of the Royal Australian Navy, sub-mariners of the Royal Navy were authorized to wear a similar insignia, the first being awarded at Ceremonial Divisions on 15 July, 1971. Nicknamed the 'Kissing Kippers', it consists of a fouled anchor above which is a St Edward's Crown. Either side of this device is an inward-facing dolphin. It measures 60mm x 21mm and has two clutch fasteners on the back. It differs from its RAN counterpart in three aspects: it is smaller, the dolphins are scaled (RAN example is smooth) and the RAN badge does not include the fouled anchor.

Unofficial versions exist in gold wire, cloth and in metal miniature. The miniature measures 45mm x 15mm, universally worn on mess kit, and an even smaller novelty type, sometimes worn on the tie, measures 19mm x 7mm. All ranks and ratings wear the same insignia which is worn on the left breast above the medal ribbons.

For officers the requirements for qualification are to successfully complete parts 1, 2, and 3 of the submarine qualification course. Part 3 includes two to six weeks at sea in a submarine depending on the branch. The total period is about six months. Requirements for ratings are similar.

Junior ratings can further be distinguished by their cap tallies. Originally they bore the submarine name prefixed by 'HMS' or the number prefixed by 'HM SUBMARINE'. This was later altered to the inscription 'HM SUBMARINE' on its own and later still to 'HM SUBMA-RINES.', the full stop being dropped in the early 1950s.

Some branch badges common to the surface fleet, but with specialist submarine sub-qualifications, have the letters 'SM' added below.

United Kingdom submarine branch sub-speciality badge, worn by ratings on the right lower sleeve 1958-64. Supplied in cloth embroidered gold on navy blue, red on navy blue and blue on white.

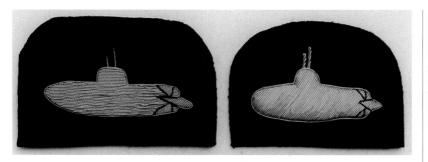

Left: official design in gold wire embroidery; right: unofficial design, probably produced for collectors well after insignia was deleted.

United Kingdom submarine qualification insignia all ranks, 15 July, 1971. In three sizes, 60mm, 45mm and 19mm.

United Kingdom, unofficial cloth badges.

United Kingdom, unofficial cloth badge.

UNITED STATES OF AMERICA

SUBMARINE SERVICE

The first United States underwater vessel was the *Turtle*, a one-man submersible propelled by a hand crank. Built in 1776, it was the first submersible to attack an enemy when it attempted to destroy Lord Howe's flagship in New York harbour. A similar vessel was built in 1801 for experimental purposes. In 1863 the Confederate Army built five rudimentary submarines. The CSS *H. L. Hunley* was the first submarine ever to destroy an enemy. Her sister the *David* destroyed a Union frigate the following year. The weapon used was a spar torpedo. Unfortunately, *David* herself was blown up in the ensuing explosion. A submarine named the *Plunger* was constructed for the Navy in 1896 but was never accepted into service.

The first submarine to actually form a part of the United States Navy was the *Holland* type SS1 in 1898. She displaced seventy-five tons, had a complement of five and was armed with an 8in dynamite gun and one 18in torpedo tube. The A Class of seven boats followed between 1901 and 1903. Four were Lake types and three were Holland types but their military characteristics were the same. They displaced 107 tons and were armed with a single 18in torpedo tube. The B and C Classes totalling eight boats were commissioned between 1906 and 1909. Slightly larger than previous boats they were armed with two 18in torpedo tubes. The forty-one boats of the D, E, F, G, H, K and L Classes built between 1909 and 1917 were all progressively larger and mounted four 18in torpedo tubes. The single M Class submarine constructed in 1915 included a 3in deck gun in its armament.

The United States entered World War I with fifty-seven submarines in service and fourteen nearing completion. War construction added over one hundred more in four classes (N, O, R, S) of which at least fifty-five were completed after the Armistice. Six U-Boats were ceded to America on the cessation of hostilities.

Between the wars the United States concentrated on the construction of 125 large ocean-going submarines designed to cruise the Pacific. Their displacement ranged from 900 to 2,000 tons, and some were armed with 6in guns.

At the outbreak of the Pacific War in 1941 the United States Navy had 112 submarines in commission and sixty-five building or on order. War construction consisted of three classes, *Gato*, *Tench* and *Balao*. All were very similar, displacing 1,525 tons and armed with ten 21in torpedo tubes, one 5in gun and one 40mm AA gun. The United States Pacific submarine force proved a formidable weapon, accounting for 1,125 Japanese merchant ships and numerous warships of all categories.

On the conclusion of the war the war-built submarines were either modernized, converted to specialist roles or transferred to friendly navies. In the 1950s a few experimental classes were built. The first post-war attack submarines, the six boats of the *Tang* Class (SS), entered service in 1951-2. They were high-speed vessels of 1,615 tons armed with eight 21in torpedo tubes. (Three improved 'tear drop' *Tang*s were later completed in 1959.) Then followed three *Barbacuda*, three *Barbel* and one *Darter* Class submarines (SS).

The world's first nuclear powered submarine, the *Nautilus*, was commissioned in 1954. It also had the distinction of being the first submarine to sail under the North Pole. A nuclear attack submarine (SSN), she displaced 3,200 tons and was armed with six 21in torpedo tubes. A near sister, the *Seawolf*, was commissioned shortly afterwards.

In 1958 two experimental nuclear submarines, the *Grayback* and *Growler*, were commissioned. They were originally armed with the Regulus guided missile but were later converted into amphibious support vehicles. At this stage it was decided that all future submarines in the United States Navy should be nuclear-powered.

The first class of SSN was designated the *Skate* Class. Improved *Nautilus/Seawolf* boats, they were completed in 1958. The *Triton*, commissioned in 1959, was a large (5,900 tons standard) nuclear-powered Radar Picket Submarine (SSR(N)). She was later converted to an SSN.

UNITED STATES OF AMERICA

The five-boat *Skipjack* Class was commissioned in 1959 to 1961. They were the first SSNs to adopt the 'tear drop' profile. They were followed by the single *Tullibee* and the thirteen-boat *Permit* Class (SSN) between 1960 and 1968. The latter boats displaced 3,750 tons standard and were armed with four 21in torpedo tubes and equipped to launch Subroc A/S torpedoes. Similarly armed, the 4,460 ton standard displacement *Sturgeon* Class (SSN) were commissioned between 1967 and 1975. A class of thirty-seven, twelve had been withdrawn by 1995 due to defence cuts. Two single-class ships *Narwhal* and *Glenard P. Lipscombe* (SSNs), were commissioned in 1969 and 1974. The *Los Angeles* Class of fifty-five large SSNs started to enter service in 1976, with the last due to be commissioned late in 1996. They have a standard displacement of 6,927 tons and are armed with torpedoes, nuclear land-attack missiles and mines.

The West's first ballistic missile submarines were the five *George Washington* Class (SSBN) which entered service in 1959/61. They displaced 5,900 tons standard and were armed with sixteen Polaris A3 missiles and four 21in torpedo tubes. They were followed by the five *Ethan Allen* (SSBN) in 1961-3, also armed with sixteen Polaris A3 missiles. The *Benjamin Franklin/Lafayette/James Madison* Classes (SSBN) were next to come into service in 1963-7. The twenty-nine submarines in these classes displaced 6,650 tons and were armed with sixteen Poseidon C3 or Trident missiles. Like all United States submarines they were also armed with torpedo tubes. All were out of service by 1995.

The *Ohio* Class (SSBN) came into service in 1979 and the total of eighteen should be in commission by 1997. Huge ships of 16,600 tons surface displacement, they are, nevertheless, about half the size of their Russian counterparts the *Typhoon* Class. The *Ohio*s were armed with twenty-four Trident missiles and four 21in torpedo tubes. This class is now the sole representative of the US Navy's strategic missile submarine fleet.

At the time of writing (1996) the United States Navy has a submarine force of fifteen SSBNs and eighty-five SSNs. Some older submarines have been converted to other roles such as platforms for special operations.

Submarine Insignia

Captain Ernest J. King (later Fleet Admiral) in 1923 suggested that it would be appropriate for submariners to have a distinguishing badge. Thus prompted, the Naval Authorities authorized a distinctive insignia on 24 March, 1924. It was intended for wear only while the individual was actually serving in submarines.

The device displayed two dolphins on waves, with a bow view of a submarine between them. The dolphins symbolized the mythical benevolence of Poseidon (Neptune) towards ships and mariners. The device was made in gold-plated metal for warrant and commissioned officers and originally had a pin fastening. Later examples were secured by clutch fasteners. The badge came in two sizes: 70mm x 20mm and 39mm x 11mm. (A miniature version measured 15mm x 5mm.) It was worn on the left breast above medal ribbons.

Enlisted men wore the same design but in cloth. For various styles of uniform it was manufactured in silver embroidery on blue, white embroidery on blue, blue embroidery on white and blue embroidery on light khaki. At this stage there was no miniature. It was worn mid-way between the wrist and elbow of the right sleeve. In 1941 permission was given for the insignia to be worn throughout the recipient's service career. New regulations in 1943 permitted enlisted men who were promoted to warrant or commissioned rank to wear the enlisted men's insignia on the left breast until they qualified as submarine officers.

In mid-1947 the enlisted men's embroidered insignia was moved from the right sleeve and repositioned to the left breast the same as for officers. On 21 September, 1950, officers were permitted to wear gold embroidered badges as well as metal. At the same time enlisted men had their insignia changed to silver plate metal, though the embroidered pattern could still be worn. Enlisted men were also granted a metal miniature in the same style as that for officers.

In the mid-1980s a printed black on light blue denim cloth 'iron-on' insignia was made available for wear on the blue working rig shirt. In 1989 this was replaced by cloth embroidered 'iron-on' badges measuring 91mm x 32mm. There are two types, in yellow for officers and light grey for enlisted men. Both are outlined in black. In 1992 a solid black embroidered cloth badge was produced for combat uniforms.

On 26 March, 1943, a new insignia was authorized. This was the Combat Patrol badge. It was issued to submariners who completed one or more patrols in which at least one enemy vessel was sunk or a special mission successfully accomplished. The device, which was made in dull grey metal, depicted a *Flying Fish* Class submarine, facing the wearer's right, below which were waves and a scroll. It measured 56mm x 13mm and had clutch or pin fastening. A miniature version was also produced. Up to three ⅛in stars could be worn on the scroll; more could be worn on either side. A gold star was added after the second patrol and each subsequent patrol. A silver star equalled five gold stars. The device was worn on the left breast below medal ribbons. It was only awarded for service in World War II. At least two variations of this badge exists.

21 May, 1943, saw the authorization of a special submarine badge for medical officers. On 11 August, 1952, it was reduced slightly in size. The design is the same as for other officers but the submarine motif is replaced by an oval device on which is a silver acorn over a gold oak leaf. It measures 70mm x 17mm and it too has a miniature version. The original version was two-piece.

On 13 July, 1950, officers assigned to submarine engineering duties were also granted a special device. Again it is the same as for other officers but the central device was then altered to a gold disc, within which was the letter 'E.' This was altered on 11 August, 1952, to a silver three-bladed ship's screw surrounded by a silver border. It measured 73mm x 17mm and also had a miniature version.

Submarine supply officers were awarded a distinctive insignia on 9 February, 1964. This too resembled the line officer's badge but the central device now took the shape of three oak leaves and acorns in gilt plate similar to the device worn on the cuff. It measured 70mm x 22mm and, like the other badges, there was also a miniature version. The Supply Corps, Medical and Engineering miniatures all measure 40mm x 10mm.

The Deterrent Patrol Badge was authorized on 28 January, 1969. It is awarded to crews in SSBNs who complete one or more three-month patrols. The device is made in dull white metal and depicts a *Lafayette* Class SSBN facing the wearer's right. In the centre there is a vertical ballistic missile supporting a nuclear symbol below which is a scroll. Up to six ⅛in stars can be fixed to the scroll. One gold star (after the initial patrol) for each patrol and one silver star for five patrols. It measures 57mm x 22mm and the miniature measures 38mm x 14mm. It has clutch fastenings and is worn on the left breast below medal ribbons.

The crews of Deep Submergence Rescue Vehicles (DSRV) were authorized to wear a special device on 6 April, 1981. It depicts a DSRV behind which is an upright trident flanked by two diving dolphins. The insignia is made in gold plate for officers and silver plate for enlisted men and is secured by clutch fasteners. It measures 36mm x 21mm. In 1971 a similar solid design with a bottom scroll bearing three stars was produced but never adopted.

A number of unofficial badges also exist. Perhaps the most famous is the 'Diesel Boats Forever' badge. This was a 'lament' for the phasing out of diesel/electric submarines in the USN. It originated with EMCS (SS) Doug Smith of the USS *Barbel* and a group of his shipmates during a cruise in the Western Pacific in 1967. One from this group, Leon

Siguerito, had been a commercial artist before he joined the Navy. Siguerito drew five sample sketches of a new pin. These were taken to the 'Thieves Alley' section of Yokosuka where the designs were discussed with Japanese craftsman. They decided on the design of a *Tang* Class submarine hull and two mermaids along with the letters 'DBF'. They had one thousand of these pins made up at $1.00 each. When they returned to Pearl Harbor the word of these pins soon got around and they were soon sold out, apparently at cost. They were evidently worn on navy bases and on leave. In 1968 the drawing was sent to the Navy Department for official approval which was never given. It seems likely that some commanders were lenient about this, pending word from the Navy. It is thought to have been worn by the crew of USS *Tigrone* in 1971. It is now sometimes seen on the chests of diesel boat veterans at annual reunions. The badge was made in gilt for officers and dull grey metal for enlisted men. They measured 66mm x 25mm and were secured with clutch fasteners. Many restrikes have been made.

Another unofficial badge takes the form of a normal submarine badge but with a bow view of a tear drop submarine in the centre. It is said to be worn by SSN crews.

The Maryland Naval Militia, which was formed in 1774 and disbanded in 1975, had a submarine badge (but no submarines) apparently for former submariners. It took the form of a normal submarine badge but the central device was replaced by the state seal.

A so-called Deep Water or Wave badge also exists. Several years ago US submariners on the Pacific Coast considered themselves to be 'Deep Water' sailors (compared to the Atlantic Coast submariners) due to the very deep regions of the Pacific Ocean. This boast was picked up by a militaria manufacturer who produced the 'Deep Water' or 'Deep Sea' dolphins. Entirely unofficial, though it may have been tolerated for wear by some individual submarine commanders, it is very similar to the official insignia but the waves are deeper and more calm and the dolphins are more animated.

As will appear evident, there is a multiplicity of design and material of USN badges, plus numerous unofficial versions. Every mode of dress seems to have been catered for.

US submarine qualification insignia in gold for line officers, 70mm and 39mm, 1924.

US submarine qualification insignia in cloth for enlisted men 1924-47. White on blue, silver embroidery on blue, blue on light khaki, and blue on white.

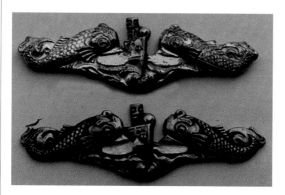

US submarine qualification insignia in silver for enlisted men, 70mm and 39mm, 1947. Bright silver and silver substitute.

US submarine qualification insignia for medical officers, authorized 1943.

US submarine qualification insignia for officers assigned to engineering duties. The original badge, authorized on 13 July, 1950, contained the letter 'E' within the circlet. This was altered to a three, bladed screw on 11 August, 1952.

US submarine qualification insignia for supply officers, authorized 1964.

US submarine qualification insignia, subdued in black metal, about the late 1970s.

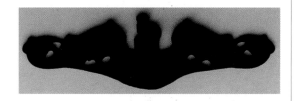

US submarine qualification insignia, 'iron-on', for enlisted men's working shirts, mid-1980s.

US embroidered cloth 'iron-on' badges about 1989 for working uniforms. Officers and enlisted men.

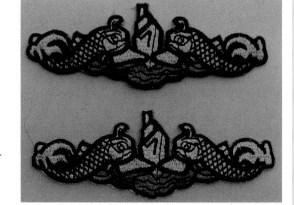

US submarine qualification insignia for officers, embroidered in yellow thread on dark blue cloth for wind-breaker jackets.

US Maryland Naval Militia insignia (obsolete).

US Deep Submergence Rescue Vehicle Badge, gold for officers and silver for enlisted men, 1981.

US Combat Patrol Badge, World War II, authorized 1943, with three gold patrol stars.

US Deterrent Patrol Badge authorized 1969, 58mm and 38mm, with one silver patrol star.

US unofficial 'Deep Water' submarine insignia.

US unofficial nuclear submarine qualification insignia.

US novelty submarine badge 'Diesel Boats Forever', gold for officers and silver for enlisted men. Stars were added for patrols. Produced in 1971 to lament the demise of conventional submarines in the US Navy.

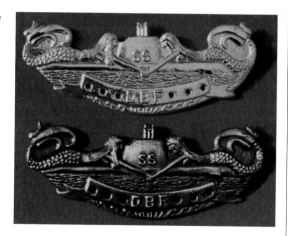

UNITED STATES OF AMERICA

VENEZUELA

SUBMARINE SERVICE

Venezuela entered the submarine field in 1960 with the purchase from the United States of the *Balao* Class (SS) USS *Tilefish*. She was renamed *Carite* and served until 1977.

In 1972 and 1973 two American *Guppy II* Class (SS) the USS *Cubera* and the USS *Grenadier* were purchased and re-named *Tiburon* and *Picua*. *Tiburon* was deleted in the early 1980s and *Picua* was relegated to harbour training in 1990.

New submarines were purchased from West Germany in 1972 and were commissioned in 1976-7. They are of the 109 Class (1300 type) (SSK) and are named *Sabalo* and *Caribe*. There are plans for two more of this class.

SUBMARINE INSIGNIA

The submarine qualification badge was authorized in 1960. It is worn in gold-plated metal for officers and silver-plated metal for ratings. The design is of a bow view of a modern submarine below which is a coloured enamel shield bearing the national arms. This is flanked either side by an inward-facing dolphin. Submarine and dolphins are supported by a representation of waves. Qualified commanding officers wear an arch of seven stars over the submarine. The standard insignia measures 71mm x 22mm (though slightly larger variations exist). They are fixed to the uniforms with clutch fasteners and worn over the left breast pocket. Honorary submarine officers, which include shore-based support staff, wear the insignia on the right breast.

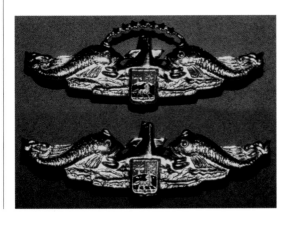

Venezuelan submarine qualification insignia. Top: commanding officers. Bottom: other officers.

Qualifications are to have attended the Submarine School and to have six months on-board service. This was extended to one year in 1989.

Venezuelan unofficial sleeve patch for non-uniform wear, Submarine Picua.

YUGOSLAVIA

SUBMARINE SERVICE

The first Yugoslav submarines were the British-built *Hrabri* and *Nebojsa* launched in 1927. They displaced 975 tons and were armed with six 21in torpedo tubes and two 4in guns. They were followed into service by the French-built *Smeli* and *Osvetnik* in 1928-9. These were 639 ton boats armed with 19.7in torpedo tubes, one 4in gun, and one 1 pdr AA gun and one machine gun.

Hrabri, Osvetnik and *Smeli* were captured by the Italians in April 1941. *Nebojsa* escaped to join Allied Naval Forces. After the war it was reported that three ex-Italian CB Class pocket submarines had been captured by Yugoslavia. *Nebojsa* was renamed *Tara* and finally deleted in 1958. She was replaced by the ex-Italian submarine *Tritone*, renamed *Sava*.

A new class of Yugoslav-built patrol submarine was constructed between 1958 and 1960 this was the *Sutjeska* Class (SS) of two boats, the *Sutjeska* and the *Neretva*. They displaced 820 tons and were armed with six 21in torpedo tubes. They were followed by three boats of the *Heroj* Class (SS): the *Heroj, Junak* and *Uskok*. The first was launched in 1968. They displace 1,068 tons and are armed with six 21in torpedo tubes.

YUGOSLAVIA

In the early 1970s a class of two-man submarines began trials. Designated the R2 *Mala* Class, they displace 1.4 tons and are swimmer delivery vehicles (SDV). They are fitted to carry two 50kg mines. A number of smaller swimmer delivery vehicles or 'wet chariots', designated R1, also became operational. These are operated by a single crewman. Five *Una* Class midget submarines have also been built. The first entered service in 1985. They have a displacement of 90 tons and can carry six mines or six swimmer delivery vehicles and have a crew of four or five. Three names have been reported: *Una*, *Zeta* and *Socha*.

The latest patrol submarines were commissioned in 1978 and 1981. These are the *Sava* Class (SS) *Sava* and *Drava*. They displace 770 tons and are armed with six 21in torpedo tubes and carry twenty mines.

In 1996 the submarine force consisted of two *Sava* Class and three *Heroj* Class patrol submarines and five *Una* Class midget submarines. There are also an unspecified number of *Mala* Class swimmer delivery vehicles. Some of these craft may have become victims of the civil war.

SUBMARINE INSIGNIA

From 1918 to 1929 the country was known as the Kingdom of Serbs, Croats and Slovenes. A metal two-piece submarine badge was authorized about 1927 depicting a silver-coloured submarine facing its wearer's left. This was fixed to a gold-coloured fouled anchor above which was a similarly coloured crown and below an escutcheon bearing the symbols of the three states. The flukes of the anchor and the crown on the left side were joined by a laurel wreath and on the right by an oak wreath, (both in gold colouring and with the submarine protruding both sides). The insignia measured 90mm x 72mm and was secured to the uniform by means of two broad blades north and south.

After 1929 a new insignia appeared. It consisted of a gold-metal-coloured laurel wreath at the top of which was a gold crown inlaid with red. A separate piece of silver metal in the form of an *Osvethik* (*Ojventnik*) Class submarine was placed over the central part and protruded either side. The submarine faced its wearer's left and on the back of both sections was the inscription '*Griesbachiknaus Zagreb*'. It was fixed to the uniform by two long vertical prong-like pins with pigtail loops at the top to provide spring. They were fixed to the bottom of the badge by simple hooks. The insignia measured 49mm x 44mm.

Kingdom of Serbs, Croats and Slovenes, submarine qualification insignia about 1927-9.

Kingdom of Yugoslavia, submarine qualification insignia, after 1929.

YUGOSLAVIA: PEOPLE'S REPUBLIC
(NOW THE FEDERATION OF SERBIA AND MONTENEGRO)

SUBMARINE INSIGNIA

The first submarine badge was authorized in 1960 and was worn by all sailors, career petty officers and officers as a recognition of submarine service. The design was of a submarine facing the wearer's left on a squat diamond-shaped background, the bottom of which had waves and at the top was a red enamelled star. Behind the diamond were crossed fouled anchors. The insignia was made in white metal and had a single screw fastener. It measures 55mm x 40mm.

In 1970 a new design was authorized for career petty officers and officers. Sailors continued to wear the original design. This new insignia consists of a laurel wreath with a red enamel star at the top and a relief silhouette of a submarine passing through the middle towards the wearer's left. Within the wreath the top part is void and the bottom is filled in with a blue and silver sea and a yellow rising sun, in the centre of which is a small black and silver stockless anchor. The reverse is smooth with a screw fastener and registration number. It measures 46mm x 38mm and is worn in the middle of the left side of the breast.

The badge is worn in silver by active officers and career petty officers after completing qualification courses and being assigned to serve in a submarine. After five years' service the badge becomes his personal property and can be worn throughout his service career. Officers and career petty officers are awarded the badge in gold after ten years' service. This badge has been produced with gold and silver wreaths.

With the demise of communism it is likely that, eventually, the red stars may be replaced by a new device.

Yugoslavian submarine qualification insignia for officers and career petty officers 1960-70 and for junior ratings from 1960 to the present.

Yugoslavian submarine qualification insignia, officers and career petty officers (silver hull) from 1970 to the present. Gold-hulled submarines are worn after ten years' service.

ACKNOWLEDGEMENTS

So much help has been given by so many people that I felt it would be better to divide them into two categories, those who contributed information of a general nature and those who contributed details concerning a particular country. The former are: AB UC S/M Keith Howe, Royal Australian Navy; Commander T. L. Nissen, Royal Danish Navy; William J. Crosby; Captain A. G. Soderlund, South African Navy; Surgeon Lieutenant-Commander Mark Smith, Royal Navy; Captain Viktor Toyka, German Navy and C. G. Vowls, Royal Naval Association.

The one exception to all these contributors is my old friend Captain Gustavo Conde of the Argentine Navy. He too was writing a book on submarine insignia and was actively researching the subject when he discovered that I was already well advanced on the same theme. Unselfishly he passed all his notes onto me; consequently this book represents our combined effort.

My appreciation also goes to Nigel Thomas for assisting with translations and to my wife 'Peggie' who typed most of the original manuscript, and to my daughter Jayne for the final print-out.

Those who have contributed details concerning individual countries are listed below. To all I extend my heartfelt gratitude.

Argentina: Captain Gustavo Conde, Argentine Navy.

Australia: Lieutenant-Commander B. W. Evans, Royal Australian Navy, Australian Submarine Liaison Officer Gosport 1986-7; AB UC S/M Keith Howe; Royal Australian Navy; J. H. Straczek, Senior Historical and Archives Officer for Director of Public Information — Navy.

Austria-Hungary: Dr Franz Kaindl, Director Military Museum Vienna.

Brazil: Captain Oscar Moreira Da Silva, Brazilian Navy, Brazilian Naval Commission Europe 1986.

Bulgaria: Colonel N. A. King, British Defence Attaché Sofia 1990.

Canada: Colonel J. G. Boulet, Director of Information Services, Department of National Defence, Ottawa, 1981; Lieutenant-Colonel L. D. Dent, Director of Information Services, Department of National Defence, Ottawa, 1986; Ms Marilyn Smith, Curator, Maritime Museum, Halifax.

Chile: Captain T. Lelaand, Royal Navy, British Defence Attaché, Santiago 1987-9.

Colombia: Ricardo Samper, Chargé d'Affaires Colombian Embassy, London 1987.

Denmark: Captain P. Kirketerp-Møller, Royal Danish Navy, Commander Danish Submarine Squadron 1988; Commander T. L. Nissen Royal Danish Navy, late captain of submarine HDMS *Narhvalen*; Colonel F. Tingleff, Royal Danish Air Force, Defence Attaché, London 1987.

Ecuador: Group Captain W. M. Watkins, Royal Air Force Defence Attaché, Quito 1988-9; Sergeant R. J. Fleming, PA to Defence Attaché, Quito 1987.

Egypt: Commanding Officer of the Egyptian Submarine Brigade; Captain J. M. Stock, Royal Navy, British Naval Attaché ,Cairo 1988. Commander Michael Maddox Royal Navy, British Naval Attaché, Cairo 1990.

Finland: Tom C. Bergroth, Finnish National Committee for Genealogy and Heraldry.

France: Vice-Admiral Doniol, French Navy, Major-General of the Navy 1987; Rear Admiral Bergot, French Navy, Assistant Chief of Staff, Operations 1987; Squadron-Leader J. Chambers, Royal Air Force, Office of the Naval Attaché, Paris 1987.

Germany: Captain Viktor Toyka, German Navy, Dr Med F. Hermann, Colonel German Army Medical Corps (Retired).

Greece: Commander D. I. Ladopoulos, Hellenic Navy, General Staff, Athens 1989; Captain C. L. MacGregor, Royal Navy, Naval and Air Attaché, Athens 1987.

India: Lieutenant-Commander N. S. Rawat, Indian Navy, Office of the High Commission for India, London 1987; Lieutenant-Commander A. V. Shiggaon, Indian Navy, Office of the High Commission for India, London 1988-9.

Indonesia: Colonel Syam Soemanagara, Indonesian Defence Attaché, London 1990; Colonel Wartono Soedarman, Commanding Officer Submarine Unit, East Fleet 1990; Warrant Officer K. Tomlinson, RAOC Office of the British Defence Attaché, Jakarta 1987.

Israel: Brigadier Y. Even, Israeli Defence Force, Defence Attaché, London 1987.

Italy: Captain Franco D'Agostino, Italian Navy, Naval Attaché, Bonn 1988, Captain G. Rondonotti, Italian Navy, Defence Attaché, London 1987; Captain Francesco Ricci, Italian Navy; Captain U. Cuzzola, Italian Navy, Naval Attaché, London 1989; Captain A. Serveri, Italian Navy, Director Naval Historical Branch; Franco Scandaluzzi, Milan.

Japan: Captain Isamu Kyoda, Japanese Maritime Self Defence Force, Defence Attaché, London 1986-9.

Netherlands: Commander A. Veentjer, Royal Netherlands Navy, Assistant Naval and Air Attaché, London 1986; Edgar Van Engeland, Netherlands.

Norway: Captain T. Nikolaisen, Royal Norwegian Navy, Defence Attaché, London 1986; Commander J. Osthus, Royal Norwegian Navy, Staff Officer to Commander Training Submarines, 1986; Commander Bjarne Tingvoll, Royal Norwegian Navy, Staff Officer to Commander Training Submarines, 1987.

Pakistan: Commander J. D. St J. Ainslie, Royal Navy, British Naval Adviser, Islamabad 1990.

Poland: Lieutenant-Colonel R. C. Eyres, 7th Gurkha Rifles, British Defence Attaché, Warsaw, 1988-9; Lieutenant-Commander R. B. Turner, Royal Navy, Assistant British Naval Attaché, Moscow and Warsaw, 1987-8; K. Barbarski, Polish Institute, London.

Portugal: Captain J. M. T. P. Germano, Portuguese Navy, Naval Attaché, London 1987-9.

Romania: Lieutenant-Colonel Peter Crocker, British Defence Attaché, Bucharest 1990; Lieutenant-Colonel Nicolaescu Gheorghe, Head of (Romanian) Foreign Liaison Section; Captain Cioenaru, Romanian Navy, 1990.

Russia/USSR: Captain J. E. Dykes Royal Navy, Defence Attaché, Moscow 1987; Commander R. B. Turner Royal Navy, Assistant Naval Attaché, Moscow and Warsaw 1988; Michael Clarke, London; Major M. Moss, TD* Intelligence Corps, London.

Saudi Arabia: Lee R. Lacey.

South Africa: Commander R. D. Stephen, South African Navy, Office of the Chief of Staff South African Defence Force, 1987-9.

Spain: Captain José Luis Carranza, Spanish Navy, Defence Attaché, London 1986; Captain P. A. Voute, Royal Navy, Services Attaché, Madrid 1988; Captain Alejandro J. Cuerdo, Spanish Navy, Defence Attaché, London 1989; Major R. D. Peters, Assistant British Defence Attaché, Madrid 1991; Captain José M. Pascual, Spanish Navy, Defence Attaché, London 1992; Lieutenant Commander J. M. Trevino, Spanish Navy.

Sweden: Captain S. Swedlund, Royal Swedish Navy, Naval Attaché, London 1987; Peter Von Busch, Director Marinmuseum, Sweden. Hans Ellerström, Sweden.

Syria: Major-General M.S. Akel, Director of Army Supply Bureau, 1989.

Taiwan: Hoh-Tu Lui, Director General, Far East Trade Office, The Hague 1987; Lieutenant-General Wang Jo-Yu, Republic of China Army, Deputy Chief of Staff for Personnel, Taiwan 1987-9.

Thailand: Rear Admiral Prida Karasuddhi, Royal Thai Navy, Director of Naval Operations, 1989; Wing-Commander H. W. Hughes, Royal Air Force, Naval and Air Attaché, Bangkok 1988.

Turkey: Commander B. Jones, Royal Navy, British Naval Attaché, Ankara 1987-8; Captain Orhan Aydin, Turkish Navy, Naval Attaché, London 1989.

USA: Harold D. Langley, Curator, Naval History Division of the Armed Forces, National Museum of American History, Smithsonian Institute, Washington DC 1988; Charles R. Steitz, USA.
Venezuela: Captain C. R. Pack, Royal Navy, British Defence Attaché, Caracas 1987; Captain Rafael I. González-Molero, Venezuelan Navy, Commander Submarine Squadron, 1987.
Yugoslavia: Colonel E. J. Everett-Heath, British Defence Attaché, Belgrade 1987; Wing-Commander M. B. M. Canavan, Royal Air Force, Naval and Air Attaché, Belgrade 1990; Colonel Slavko Jovic, Yugoslav Army, Foreign Liaison Section, Federal Secretariat for National Defence, Belgrade 1988.

Acknowledgements are due to the following for supplying illustrations:
Commander Danish Submarine Squadron: page 36 (top).
Commander T. L. Nissen: page 36 (centre left).
Marine Nationale: page 45 (top and lower left).
K. Howe: pages 61 (top), 63 (top).
Portuguese Navy: page 98.
Royal Thai Navy: page 126 (top).

BIBLIOGRAPHY

To the author's knowledge, no other book has been published commercially on the subject of submarine insignia. The following list, therefore comprises books that are of interest for those wishing to read more on the subject of submarines generally.

Botting, Douglas, *The U-Boats* (Time-Life Books, 1979)

Compton-Hall, Richard, *Submarine Boats* (Conway Press Ltd, 1983)

Gunston, Bill, *Submarines in Colour* (Blandford Press Colour Series, 1976)

Jane's Fighting Ships (Jane's Information Group Ltd, published annually).

Navies of the Second World War (series) (MacDonald & Co [Publishers] Ltd, 1965-91)

Showell, J. P. Mallmann, *U-Boats under the Swastika* (MacDonald and Jane's, 1977)

Warship series (Ian Allan, 1968)

Watts, Anthony J., *Allied Submarines and Axis Submarines* (MacDonald and Jane's, 1977)